D1552550

Customer Service in Libraries

Best Practices

Edited by
Charles Harmon
Michael Messina

THE SCARECROW PRESS, INC.
Lanham • Toronto • Plymouth, UK
2013

Published by Scarecrow Press, Inc.
A wholly owned subsidiary of The Rowman & Littlefield Publishing Group, Inc.
4501 Forbes Boulevard, Suite 200, Lanham, Maryland 20706
www.rowman.com

10 Thornbury Road, Plymouth PL6 7PP, United Kingdom

British Library Cataloguing in Publication Information Available

Library of Congress Cataloging-in-Publication Data

Customer service in libraries : best practices / edited by Charles Harmon, Michael Messina.
    pages cm
  Includes bibliographical references and index.
  ISBN 978-0-8108-8748-0 (pbk.) — ISBN 978-0-8108-8749-7 (ebook) 1. Public services (Libraries)—United States. 2. Customer services—United States. I. Harmon, Charles, 1960- II. Messina, Michael.
  Z711.C88 2013
  025.50973—dc23   2012044861

∞™ The paper used in this publication meets the minimum requirements of American National Standard for Information Sciences—Permanence of Paper for Printed Library Materials, ANSI/NISO Z39.48-1992. Printed in the United States of America.

Contents

Introduction

AUDRA CAPLAN

Former President of the Public Library Association

Last week, the business section of my local newspaper, the *Baltimore Sun*, featured an article on how giant home-improvement chains are focusing on building customer service initiatives. The article specifically cited Home Depot and Lowe's. I had been in a Home Depot recently and expected to have the same disorienting experience I always have when shopping there, but much to my astonishment, the store had a sales representative at the end of almost every aisle. I was asked numerous times if I needed assistance, and when I responded that I did, the person who helped me walked me to the location I needed and then made recommendations for products based on my specific needs. Needless to say, I was a very happy customer and will return with much less trepidation. It turns out that this is the result of a major initiative called "Customers First." Home Depot employees have been retrained and are required to spend 60% of their time helping customers. Their previous focus had been on stocking shelves and cleaning. Over the last year, the price of their shares has increased 80%, and their sales have gone up dramatically. At Lowe's, the company outfitted all of its stores with wi-fi and supplied 25 iPhones for associates to help customers with their shopping. Now customers can look up required materials and give accurate dimensions so that products can be identified immediately and bought on the spot. Both these initiatives are examples of best practices in customer service and can easily be translated to what we do in libraries.

In my opinion, creating a culture of excellent customer service in libraries is the most important factor in our future survival. In his article "Am I Obsolete? How Customer Service Principles Ensure the Library's Relevance," Mark Bernstein suggests that an ever-increasing number of people will question whether libraries will be necessary in the future as the use of technology expands and increases. He states that how we can ensure that we and our libraries do not become obsolete is to provide customer service: "Without the service mission and the people who provide that service libraries are nothing more than a warehouse."[1]

Ask employees of any public library why the library exists, and most of them are likely to say that we're here to serve our patrons/customers. Still, how we define and deliver customer service differs widely from one library to another. Some believe that the quality of the work we now provide is enough, while others believe that customer service is the most important thing that we do, and it is provided at every level of the organization. Exceptional libraries demonstrate their commitment to their customers in everything that they do. The first gauge of having a customer service culture goes beyond individual encounters to building mission, vision, values, and policies around assessing and fulfilling customer's needs. The first sentence in the Brooklyn Public Library's customer service policy states, "Customer Service is an integral part of the Brooklyn Public Library's service to Brooklyn's diverse population."[2] The policy then proceeds to lay out all of the tenets that define excellent customer service that the staff will provide.

Strangely, great customer service continues to be the exception rather than the rule. Generally, I am unable to get through a day without experiencing a bad customer service encounter. I know from my 32 years of working in public libraries that we are just as capable of providing poor customer service as any other service agency.

In this age of fast-paced change, providing superior customer service becomes more and more challenging. To survive, libraries must provide service that reflects customers' changing expectations and needs. More than ever, our customers can now choose where they go for information, and the library is likely not to be the first choice. I have heard from library directors and librarians in all types of libraries that in recent years that there has been a decline in the number of reference questions they are recording. Customers have more options than ever before and less loyalty. They want services fast, easily accessible, around the clock, in person, online, and with value added from whoever will provide it to them. We have to find a way to keep our customers, and that means that we must provide a more satisfactory experience than our competition. Moreover, if we don't provide that experience, then e-mail and social networking opportunities make it easy for customers to broadcast their dissatisfaction. Of course, if we do provide an exceptional experience, we can touch thousands of people through these same channels. A recent post on Facebook came from a young man whose grandmother was dying and had expressed a craving for Panera's clam chowder. The man called his local Panera on a Monday, knowing that the chowder was served only on Fridays.

The manager responded quickly, saying that she would make some that day to fill this request. She provided the soup and an unexpected box of cookies free of charge. You can imagine how appreciative the family was for this service. When I observed the post, it had already received 678,824 likes on Facebook in the space of just 2 days.

Since I have been given the opportunity to write this introduction, I am going to take the liberty to use it as a bully pulpit. I would like to suggest some basic concepts that I believe ensure exceptional customer service in organizations.

Start at the top. If the CEO, director, or administrators do not understand that quality service is a basic performance expectation of all members of the staff, then it will not permeate the rest of the organization. The entire organization must be focused on what the customer wants. Customer feedback should be taken seriously and reviewed in a positive and nondefensive manner, and changes should be implemented if the feedback improves service. For this culture to thrive, the administration must have the passion to communicate this message throughout the organization.

Customers are the reason for work, not an interruption. It is very easy to lose sight of the importance of the customer and to become consumed by day-to-day tasks. Good customer service should be a priority for everyone. I joined the board of a volunteer organization that ran a shop that sells handmade crafts. The first time I visited the store, the manager (we had only one paid employee) sat behind the counter looking at the computer screen. She never looked up, never greeted me, and never asked me if I needed assistance. She lasted about 2 more months and was replaced by someone who clearly loved people. She not only greeted customers but gave them a brief history of the organization and its mission. She demonstrates a genuine interest in meeting the customers' needs. She has made the effort to become familiar with the tastes and preferences of several regular visitors, and she shows them new items she thinks they might like. Unsurprisingly, sales have tripled since she has taken over.

For library staff, it is very easy to get absorbed in a report while at a service desk or to work on the collection and never look up. Never ignore a customer. If you are helping someone, always acknowledge the person waiting and explain that you will be with him or her as soon as possible. No one likes feeling invisible.

On the flip side, I have watched staff in libraries where I have worked provide service that is above and beyond—not only in small branches but in large busy agencies. I watched numerous staff at the library system where I was director spend long periods of time helping people to apply for jobs and unemployment online in addition to offering a new fiction title that they make like. Many of these same customers came out to advocate for us during a bad budget year.

Hire the right people! If you take nothing else away from this introduction, please remember this. My mantra as a director was that you can teach people skills, but it is far harder to change attitudes. People with experience may not always be the best candidates. Not everyone understands what good customer service looks like, and many don't have the personalities for it. You have to like people to want to work in a service profession. We hired a young man in his 20s for the position of web manager. We had candidates who had many more years of experience. This young man had the skills we needed, but more important, he exhibited a warm personality and maturity beyond his years. He has proven over and over again that he understands what excellent service looks like with customers both internal and external. He is always thinking of ways to improve virtual and web services and is infinitely patient when explaining new web applications and resources to people. He also has volunteered for numerous community outreach events that go way beyond his job description. His interpersonal skills have helped the library bridge new partnerships and cement relationships with a number of stakeholders.

Train, train, and train! Train all parties in the culture as soon as they are hired. Include a customer service component in your orientation package. Talk to new employees about the values of the organization and the importance of excellent customer service at every level.

Cross-train staff so that customers can be assisted as quickly as possible. There is nothing more infuriating than having a problem and getting shuffled to employees that are not empowered to assist.

Offer continuous customer service training for staff even after they are providing great service. Equally important is to make sure that staff members have opportunities for professional development on new products and services. We introduced e-books into our collection a few years ago, trained most of the librarian staff on how to download them, and directed them to help customers on the phone and in person. A few months later, we discovered that they were directing customers who had questions about e-books to one librarian at a specific branch because they deemed him the "expert." This meant that all of our customers were being redirected to someone in another location who might not even be working at the time he was needed. We went back and provided additional training to all appropriate staff until everyone was comfortable answering questions and demonstrating how to download e-books.

People may complain about too much customer service training, but in reality, there is never enough. The staff are the most important component of customer service, from delivery drivers to catalogers, selectors, and reference librarians. We can't sell great customer service unless we are able to deliver it.

Empower your staff to serve. Never let staff cite rules that have to be followed. Allow staff the latitude to make decisions, to take action to provide exceptional customer service, and to resolve issues. This saves the customers from having to go to numerous people for a resolution to their problem; it also relays to the staff that you trust them to make the right decisions. Having said this, you must support those decisions if the staff are to feel truly empowered. Weigh the cost and benefit of remedying the situation as opposed to enforcing the rules. Everyone has read of a study that reports how customers are very likely to tell friends about bad experiences and far less likely to report good ones. We also read that customers will complain to their friends but not to the business or agency that provided the service. These reports ring true to us because we recognize that behavior in ourselves. Is it worth the bad publicity just to stick to your guns? Flexibility is always a key factor in resolving issues. There is almost always a way to satisfy the customer. Give the employee the power to do so.

Treat employees and customers both with respect. It is important to sincerely model the behavior you would like staff to replicate.

Take responsibility for failures and shortcomings; don't point the finger and don't shoot the messenger. When dealing with a customer service failure, acknowledge the problem and the library's responsibility to fix it. Apologize and figure out the solution no matter whose fault the problem is. It fans the flames when customers are upset and they have to go through an aggravating process of getting you to accept the blame. Make it simple for customers to complain, and value those complaints. How else will we improve?

Just say yes! When you receive a request, tell the customer, internal or external, that you can do it (as long as it is reasonable), and then figure out a way to make it happen. If you can't find a solution, find someone who can. Think before you blurt out a negative response. This proves that you were listening and want to help.

Don't just try to meet your customers' needs. Try to exceed their expectations. Award-winning libraries anticipate their customers' needs by providing new services that meet those needs. The more you know your customers, the better you become at this. Think about what you can provide your customers that is totally unexpected. The library where I used to work recently won a grant for an exhibit on the history of transportation in the area. Knowing the interests of its community, it also organized an antique car show and had hundreds of car owners agree to participate. The show was a huge success; it received accolades from everyone, including the elected officials, and received huge press coverage. Almost all voiced pleasant surprise that this was a library endeavor.

* * *

Providing great customer service certainly involves more than these basic concepts. Everything that we do has customer service components, whether it is providing clear and understandable communications or a welcoming physical environment. More and more, we are called on to handle emergency situations in the library or help out in a community disaster. Some of the best examples of exceptional customer service have arisen from these events. Library staff have stepped up and provided shelter, computers for communication, and services to many traumatized constituents. The response after Hurricane Katrina and recent tornados are a few examples. Recently in my community, we experienced a *derecho*, a storm that caused tremendous damage and almost a million power outages across the state during a week where the average temperatures were verging on 100 degrees. Libraries with power remained open extra hours to provide a cool place for people to stay, provided outlets to charge portable devices, instructed customers in how to access the library's wi-fi service, handed out bottles of water, and so on. A neighboring library branch was inundated with people trying to stay cool. The staff there organized impromptu story hours and activities for the children to keep them occupied. All of these are examples of staff going above and beyond to provide great service in very trying situations.

The following chapters of this book will provide a number of best practices in customer service—from overall customer service training to specific areas, including acquisitions, children's services, and technology. There is nothing magical about providing excellent customer service; it just takes the right people, the right philosophy, and the passion to make it a reality.

NOTES

1. Mark P. Bernstein, "Am I Obsolete? How Customer Service Principles Ensure the Library's Relevance," http://www.aallnet.org/main-menu/Publications/spectrum/Archives/Vol-13/pub-sp0811/pub-sp0811-obsolete.pdf.

2. Brooklyn Public Library, "Customer Service Policy," http://www.brooklynpubliclibrary.org/policy/customer-service.

Service Is Personal: The Howard County Library System Customer Service Program

Lewis Belfont
Howard County Library System

THE PHILOSOPHY OF EXCEPTIONAL CUSTOMER SERVICE

The Howard County Library System (HCLS) has been tremendously successful. In a 5-year period, from 2005 to 2010, borrowing and attendance at classes and events doubled. In the most recent fiscal year, customers borrowed 7.1 million items, or 24 per capita, the highest in Maryland. Other usage statistics are similarly impressive:

- 2 million research interactions,
- 3 million physical visits, and
- 6 million virtual visits.

A major reason for the HCLS's success has been exceptional customer service. A customer's remark captures the appeal of extraordinary service: "Everyone knows me by sight, if not by name, greets me warmly, offers assistance, and makes fabulous recommendations. If I had to limit the list to just one, I'd say their wizardry at getting me what I needed, no matter how great the challenge." Approachable and engaging, knowledgeable and caring staff, who are dedicated to customers' success and are creators of memorable educational experiences, inspire customers' fierce loyalty.

The philosophy of exceptional customer service infuses service with a distinctive sense of purpose that connects with customers' lifestyles and self-images, further strengthening their identification with and loyalty to the library. Service becomes a cause, and service providers are passionate crusaders. For the HCLS, the cause, expressed in its mission statement, is "high quality public education for all ages." Public "education empowers people, enabling success at every stage in life." The HCLS's vision is to "advance the economy" through public education and enhance the quality of life. Exceptional customer service advances public education. Staff envision themselves as public educators who are dedicated customer advocates, using their knowledge and skills to leverage resources in the library's collection for customers' success, forming partnerships in knowledge creation and dissemination. As libraries struggle to retain and attract customers in the wake of the digital revolution, personalized attention and customized assistance, combined with a distinctive sense of purpose, clearly differentiate libraries from their digital competitors and are compelling reasons to continue visiting the library.

WHY CREATE A NEW PHILOSOPHY OF CUSTOMER SERVICE?

Pragmatic and focused on results, with neither interest in nor patience for exploring the meaning of their experiences, the HCLS service specialists were mostly unaware of the beliefs motivating their service behaviors. A new service philosophy could not succeed if it was imposed by management. Staff had to discover for themselves the limitations of their beliefs and practices to become motivated to develop new beliefs and habits. The first steps in creating the new philosophy of customer service were to engage staff in

- identifying their service beliefs,
- mapping the interrelationship of beliefs,
- explicating their meaning, and
- assessing their impact on service.

Beginning with supervisors and managers (the custodians of the current philosophy of service) and later expanding to include front-line staff, facilitated discussion was conducted over several months to explore their implicit beliefs about themselves, customers, and service. The advantage of this approach over individual interviews is that unfolding group dynamics separated individual opinions from cultural beliefs, permitting the identification of shared beliefs. The first discussion began with a definition of the "philosophy of customer service" as the "why" of service, the purpose that informs what we do for customers and how we do it. These beliefs, participants were informed, are not explicitly articulated in written documents, such as policy and procedure manuals or mission and vision statements. They can't be directly observed, but their influence on service is recognizable. Our task was to examine current service practices and outcomes to identify these beliefs and explore their influence.

Scenarios based on actual customer service incidents were the topics of discussion. Each scenario invited participants to become the service provider solving a service problem. Participants were instructed to focus on "what is actually done" rather than "what should be done" to solve this and a host of service problems. Strategies, methods, and solutions proffered by participants revealed their beliefs. Open-ended questions surfaced participants' assumptions and values. Three initial questions framed the discussions:

- Why is the customer in the scenario behaving this way?
- What does she expect you to do for her and why?
- How do you know your interpretation of her wants is accurate?

Probing questions identified and clarified assumptions and values implied in participants' statements:

- What do you think caused the problem?
- What motivates the customers?
- How do you justify or explain your solution?
- What facts guided your choices and decisions?
- How do these beliefs and values relate to the library's mission and vision?

Change began the moment that participants' questioned their experiences. As they shared solutions to service problems, circulation specialists, for example, realized that they were unaware of many of the assumptions they employed to sort through issues, manage customers' expectations, and negotiate solutions. They discovered how assumptions operate automatically and unconsciously and often work together to form scripts they follow when assisting customers. Metaphors, images, and expressions from their answers were recorded and organized into an outline of the current philosophy of service, focusing on assumptions defining

- the essential purpose or business of the library,
- their roles as service providers,
- the meaning of customer satisfaction,
- customer service standards, and
- customers' privileges and responsibilities.

When the outline was distributed to participants, the conversation shifted from discovery to assessment.

The new question posed to staff was "How well does the philosophy of service achieve the mission and vision of the library?" Once again, the facilitator's questions encouraged staff to form their own conclusions:

- What are customers' service expectations?
- How often do we meet or exceed them?
- What is the role of our service philosophy in meeting or exceeding customers' service expectations?

Circulation specialists, for instance, realized that their beliefs about protecting the library's collections from customers, not circulation policies, were barriers to the responsive service desired by customers. We learned that we operated from many philosophies, often at cross-purpose, and the task ahead was to create one philosophy of service.

DISCOVERING THE FOUNDATIONS
OF EXCEPTIONAL CUSTOMER SERVICE

Despite the multiplicity of philosophies of customer service, HCLS service specialists often exceeded customers' expectations for personal attention and individualized service. The customer service team—eight customer service and research staff led by the head of customer service—was charged with developing a consistent customer-focused philosophy of service. The team began by examining examples of exceptional customer service to identify the beliefs contributing to success. Figure 1.1 is the questionnaire we developed to facilitate the team's discoveries.

Two of the first three questions sought to identify the rewards that service providers received from exceptional service. The goal was for participants to recognize that exceptional service produces positive, self-affirming outcomes for themselves. Knowing that one's expertise benefited another person and contributed to the library's success strengthens one's satisfaction, sense of accomplishment, and self-efficacy. Feeling a customer's happiness, excitement, pleasure, and delight leads one to feel similar emotions. Experiencing a customer's trust or respect generates positive energy that service specialists seek to recapture with subsequent customers. These questions reminded participants that positive personal connection with customers was a worthwhile service objective.

The goal of the fourth question and subsequent discussion was to restore customers' humanity. Service specialists recognized that their service expectations were the same as library customers': The need for recognition, ac-

EXCEPTIONAL CUSTOMER SERVICE

Instructions

Please answer the questions by yourself or with a partner. Partners are to take
turns interviewing each other and share their responses. Please take notes on
the form.

After you answer the first three questions, each member of the group will share
their stories of exceptional service.

We will do the same after completing the fourth question.

We will then explore, as a group, how values, such as respect, fairness and trust,
contributed to exceptional customer service.

Your dream of future service may be expressed in writing, a picture or music.

Introduction

Exceptional customer service—always meeting or exceeding the expectations
of customers—is the goal of every service provider in Howard County Library
System. Whether it is recommending a title, helping students answer their
homework questions, leading book discussions, developing the reading skills
of children, adjusting library policy to accommodate a customer's needs, or
assisting job seekers with preparing their resumes on public computers, making
a difference in the lives of customers motivates us to the highest levels of
achievement.

Think about a time when your service to a customer was exceptional. This could
be a time when you delighted a customer and made their day better, established
a strong personal connection, or helped someone transform information into
knowledge.

Questions

1. What did you do that allowed this moment of exceptional customer service to
   take place?
2. What was the customer's reaction?
3. How did the interaction make you feel?
4. Next, recall when you were a customer and experienced exceptional service.
   • What did the service provider do make your experience memorable?
   • How did the experience make you feel?
   • Did you use the business or the individual's services again?
5. How did values, such as respect or fairness and others, contribute to both
   examples of exceptional service?
6. Drawing from your answers to the previous questions, write a dream/vision of
   future service when you are most engaged with and connected to customers,
   using your knowledge and skills to co-create the best possible library
   experience.

Figure 1.1.   Our staff questionnaire.

ceptance, and belonging, as well as service that was valued added, motivated their interactions with service providers. In a genuine helping relationship, service providers employ their knowledge and skills to assist fellow humans, not customers. Removing the label of "customer" will attune service specialists to the individuality and aspirations of each person to be assisted.

The stories also revealed that implicit conceptions of fairness, respect, trust, commitment, understanding—to name a few values—guided participants' behavior toward customers. Values functioned as their implicit standards for creating mutually beneficial interpersonal relationships. Values specified how they would treat others and how they preferred to be treated in return. The conversation turned to identifying the core values always present at times of exceptional service. Two values—respect and fairness—were identified to be essential to all relationships. The next step was for participants to define each value as observable behaviors. Respect became

- friendly greeting,
- open body language,
- direct eye contact,
- undivided attention,
- conversational tone of voice,
- exchanging information,
- active listening (probing, clarifying, verifying, paraphrasing), and
- gracious problem solving.

The expectation was established that these behaviors are to be always modeled when assisting customers. Operationally defining values also produced a list of operating assumptions, or guidelines that reinforce the aforementioned behaviors and function as scripts for collecting and interpreting customer information:

- Value customers.
- Always satisfy customers' human needs.
- Assume that customers value the library.
- Customers are motivated by enlightened self-interest.
- Positive reinforcement produces positive results.
- Customers are trustworthy unless facts, not inferences, demonstrate otherwise.
- Give customers the benefit of the doubt.
- Create face-saving opportunities.
- Do not judge customers; instead, ask questions to understand their perspective and get the facts.

- All customers' needs are equal.
- All problems are solvable to each customer's satisfaction.

One of service specialists' main responsibilities as a collaborator is to ensure equal access to library resources for all customers. Fairness is a core value because library service involves the equitable allocation of scarce resources. Circulation policies are the primary means to ensure that all customers have equal opportunities to borrow and use library materials. The traditional library definition of fairness is procedural. Fairness is the equal application of library policies in all situations without exception. This means, for example, that every customer gets two renewals and no more when policy sets the limit at two. Equal application of circulation policy may produce equal outcomes, but it will not satisfy customers whose wants and needs conflict with those policies. They expect service specialists to act as arbiters and adjust policies on their behalf.

Accordingly, fairness became a decision-making process involving the identification of the particular implications of a customer's request for other customers and the library. The most fundamental operating assumption is that each customer's needs, wants, and tastes are to be valued, respected, and fulfilled whenever possible. Acting from this premise, service providers are to collect as much information as possible as the first step. A brief interview may reveal that the customer requesting a third renewal, for example, wants to finish reading the book for next week's class. Guided by the new definition of fairness, the service provider's next step is to assess supply and demand. A check of the catalog revealed that a few copies were borrowed, no copies were requested, and many copies remained on the shelves to satisfy any potential demand. Then the service specialist applied the following criterion: An exception to library policy is permissible if the advantage to one customer does not create a significant disadvantage to other customers. In this case, the customer could get extra time to finish reading the book because extending the loan does not impose a burden on library users. A fair decision balances each customer's wants and needs with the interests of all customers and the goals of the HCLS. An exception will not be made if the decision is not in the best interests of most customers and the library. If a policy can't be adjusted, service specialists will explain the reasons and offer other options to customers. Respect and fairness are the foundation of the philosophy of exceptional customer service, enabling service specialists to identify right from wrong. It is for this reason that the philosophy of exceptional customer service is also known as values-based customer service.

WRITING THE PHILOSOPHY OF EXCEPTIONAL CUSTOMER SERVICE: *SERVICE IS PERSONAL*

This material was organized into *Service Is Personal*, a booklet written in 2002 to introduce staff to the philosophy and methods of values-based customer service. It explains in 10 pages the origins and purpose of this philosophy of customer service, illustrates how it operates, and instructs staff in its use. It has become, over time, the library's customer service textbook. Supervisors, for example, use it to introduce the library's service expectations to new staff. It is frequently consulted when designing new services, revising policies, or implementing new procedures. It was updated in 2012 to incorporate the library's new mission, vision, and organizational values, but the philosophy itself remained unchanged, a testament to its strength and enduring value.

Service Is Personal is narrated in the third-person plural to reflect staff's authorship. Although written by the customer service team, *Service Is Personal* draws on the experiences and insights of all staff and represents their collective wisdom. Its narrator speaks directly to readers in a conversational style to engage their intellect and imagination in understanding and appreciating values-based customer service. The narrator starts with the definition of the philosophy of exceptional service as "the lens through which we perceive our colleagues and customers, the map that orients our actions, and the system of meaning that provides us with purpose and goals." The metaphors give physical substance to an otherwise abstract concept, making it easily understandable and vividly establishing the direct connection of ideas and beliefs to actions and outcomes. In addition, the practical consequences of the service philosophy are identified. It is a tool to facilitate successful customer service, providing service specialists with "an integrated, consistent basis for interpreting policies and procedures, making judgments and decisions, and providing exceptional service." Informed that *Service Is Personal* "outlines how a customer service philosophy can assist us in achieving the vision of Howard County Library System," the narrator directly informs readers that their responsibility is to become adept practitioners:

> When we put on our name badges and step behind a Customer Service or Research Desk, we personify our Customer Service philosophy. We prize its values, operate from its assumptions, and model its behaviors. We achieve our values through incomparable customer service.

The primary component is the HCLS's organizational values, defined as "enduring beliefs about what is important, worthwhile and valuable to us." The values, which staff identified as their guiding principles, were respect, inclusiveness, unity, assertive communication, continuing education, exceptional customer service, and progress. Operating assumptions, which were derived from values, are identified as "guidelines to which we refer whenever we assist customers and interpret policies, solve customer service problems, or handle unfamiliar situations." Behavior—defined as decision making, problem solving, conversation, and other service-related activities—is the final component. The objective for each service specialist is to ensure the consistency of their behaviors, operating assumptions, and values.

"To consistently exceed customers' expectations," readers are instructed, "each of us must adopt the following operating assumptions, which help us interpret customers' behaviors and clarify our goals." Operating assumptions are identified as principles to consult when assisting customers and controls to keep in check "personal tendencies that that can hinder our ability to achieve our values." In this context, they also function as performance expectations identifying how service specialists are to achieve the library's mission and vision through their conduct:

1. Value customers' needs.
2. Encourage customers to be responsible library users.
3. Believe customers will return our respect.
4. Assume customers are trustworthy unless their behavior indicates otherwise.
5. Do not judge customers.
6. Always deliver excellence.
7. Problems are solvable to each customer's satisfaction.

The operating assumptions of values-based service explain customers, give meaning to service, and purpose to service specialists. They identify appropriate service behaviors and outcomes to be achieved. They are methods and strategies of communication that facilitate learning and mutual understanding. They are principles enabling service specialists to make informed decisions. Many operating assumptions come directly from the expectations of customers further strengthening the bonds of collaboration.

STAFF REACTION

When it was distributed in 2002 to HCLS staff, *Service Is Personal* generated three types of response from service specialists. Some embraced values-based customer service because it affirmed their beliefs and validated their practices. Others resisted values-based service because it contradicted their values and undermined their practices. Many were anxious about their new authority and uncertain of their knowledge and skills. Resistance and anxiety were common among customer service specialists, many of whom thought that their primary allegiance was to the library's collections, not customers. Circulation policies and procedures were instruments to protect library resources and regulate customer behavior. Service was conceived as the application of policies and procedures with scant attention to its human dimension. Rules structured relationships with customers, who were viewed through the lens of suspicion and mistrust. When service problems arose for which there was no explicit policy, circulation specialists deduced a solution from the most relevant one. When borrowers' needs and circulation policies conflicted, circulation specialists almost always ruled in favor of the policy. Comfortable with applying rather than interpreting policies and content to refer customers with special requests to their supervisors, these service specialists saw the world in black and white and were not persuaded by Service Is Personal to modify either their beliefs or their behaviors.

Customer service specialists who were resistant to values-based customer service were targeted for special attention from their supervisors. Customer service supervisors were early adapters and passionate advocates of values-based customer service because it transformed customers into allies rather than adversaries, which made work more enjoyable and engaging, enhanced their reputations and standing among library managers, and announced the importance of circulation services to the mission and vision of the library. Supervisors communicated and reinforced work performance expectations based on the philosophy of customer service at every opportunity. Informal conversations, staff meetings, and performance reviews provided opportunities to encourage and reward the adaptation of the behaviors and objectives of values-based customer service by their direct reports. New performance standards, formal and informal incentives, and social pressure combined to breakdown resistance. Actually experiencing the positive emotions associated with creating exceptional customer service—delight, accomplishment, satisfaction, and pride—was the last step in converting customer service specialists into practitioners of values-based customer service.

2

Technically Speaking: Technology Planning as the Backbone of Good Customer Service

KAREN C. KNOX
The Orion Township Public Library

Technology plays an increasingly important role in libraries. If you work in a library, likely one of the first things you do when you get to work is log-in to a computer, perhaps check e-mail, or view the online calendar of events for the day. A library's core business is built with an integrated library system (ILS), which manages the library's ability to meet the needs of the staff and public users by managing the library's patrons and materials database. The network in the library allows the ILS and other systems to communicate with one another. The Internet connection allows the library to share information with the world outside the library building. The hardware and software create the technology services in the library. The library staff and vendors support and maintain the technology that keeps everything running in the library. Without all of these pieces, libraries are unable to provide the highest level of technology services to our users.

For a number of years, libraries have been struggling with declining budgets and increasing demands. It is challenging to maintain a solid technology infrastructure when available resources are insufficient. Libraries are forced to prioritize services, and unfortunately, due the high costs, technology often receives insufficient resources. However, if the technology needs are put on the back burner for too many years, the cost to improve things continues to increase. It is much easier to maintain the technology infrastructure continuously than to try to tackle it all at once. So the ultimate goal is to establish a solid technology foundation and continue to maintain it over time in manageable pieces.

It can be overwhelming to establish that solid foundation, especially if there is a great deal of work to be done to get there, but I hope that sharing my experience shows that it can be accomplished. I was hired at the Rochester

11

Hills Public Library in November 2005. When I was hired, there were very few resources available to provide any history or documentation of the existing infrastructure. So I relied on my previous experience and knowledge as I explored the equipment. One of the first things that jumped out at me was that the antivirus software had not been updated in months . . . and that is never a good thing. So I started to investigate there. Unfortunately, I discovered there was a lot more going on than an out-of-date antivirus solution. It would be impossible to fix the antivirus software without first fixing the underlying network problems—and from there, I started my list.

In December, the library signed a contract with Polaris Library Systems to migrate to a new ILS, and I was responsible for making that happen. As I researched the Polaris system, I learned how closely it integrated into a Windows network environment. Therefore, the basic Windows management tools had to be functioning properly for Polaris to work as necessary. When the contract was signed, there was work to be done before that would happen. So certain priorities on my list were rising to the top.

MAKING THE PLAN

When managing technology in a library, it is very important to have a technology plan that outlines the projects and all the important resources needed to be successful. In my plan for the Rochester Hills Public Library, I defined the projects, the timeline for each, and the resources necessary for completion. This is not a simple task, but the more complete the plan is, the easier the implementation will be. Each project in the plan should align with the library's mission, vision, and values and be able to help the library accomplish its goals.

When it comes to technology in libraries, I feel strongly that libraries should embrace technology for the purpose of furthering service. It may be more enjoyable to embrace the latest new gadget because it is fun, but if the gadget does not fill a need for the library, then there is no reason to create a project just so you can play with it. The same is true for any type of new technology. However, there are plenty of library needs that can be fulfilled by new technology, and sometimes it is one of the fun technologies that can be most helpful. Just remember that your library's technology projects should start with a need that is solved with technology, rather than the other way around.

To write a technology plan, start with your library's goals and objectives. For example, the Rochester Hills Public Library has goals for public service, and one objective is to "maintain and upgrade computer equipment to provide consistent and efficient access to electronic projects and services." This objective can be achieved by keeping hardware for our public computers current, among other projects.

The bulk of the technology plan is goals, objectives, and projects. However, each project also has a timeline that indicates when the project will be completed. Your entire technology plan should cover a time frame of no more than 3 years, as it is very difficult to anticipate where technology will be more than 3 years in the future.

Once all the goals, objectives, and projects have been defined, your technology plan should include an inventory of what the library's current technology infrastructure contains: hardware, software, network equipment, servers, printers, and so on. Creating this inventory for your library is a helpful step to outline exactly what you have and, from there, to define what you need. When I was creating this at the Rochester Hills Public Library, it became a tool that I referred to frequently as I implemented projects, to determine the details of what we needed.

The last three sections of the technology plan include staffing and training, budget requirements and projections, and evaluation. For any technology project, the library must define and include the staffing and training needs to get the project off the ground and keep it supported. This section gives an overview of what level of staffing is available and what types of training are necessary to complete the plan. The budget requirements define what resources must be available to implement the projects in this plan. There will be financial resources needed to purchase hardware and software, and there will be staffing and time resources needed to get the work done. It is very important to include all of this in your technology plan so that it is clear what can and cannot be done if the resources are available or not. Finally, the section of the plan that is most often overlooked involves evaluation: How will you know if your plan is successful? How will you evaluate the projects that you complete and determine if they improve the library's service? How will you learn from any mistakes that come up along the way? After all the work you put into the plan and implementation, don't cheat yourself out of the benefits of the time needed to do the evaluation.

I have posted a sample technology plan on my website that you are welcome to review: http://www.karencknox.com/documents/Sample%20Technology%20Plan.pdf.

CONNECTIVITY

When I started investigating the environment at the Rochester Hills Public Library, I learned that there were some large problems with the infrastructure and network. The network is the series of cables and equipment that tie all the computers. Without a properly configured network, the computers are unable to communicate with one another and therefore know only about the software that runs locally on each computer.

However, most systems rely on multiple computers communicating with one another or at least communicating with a central server. At a basic level, this is how the Internet works. If you want to access the Internet from a computer in the library, it must be connected to a network and allowed to communicate to the huge network (the Internet) outside the library. Conversely, the library's network must be connected to the Internet for users (computers) outside the library to communicate with servers inside the library, which might include your online catalog.

So the network is important, and it must be stable and reliable to provide high-quality customer service. At a minimum, libraries provide computers with access to their catalog systems so that customers can research and locate items within the library's collection. Therefore, the computers in the library must be on a network to use resources that live on servers inside the library, such as the library's collection database.

Over a decade ago, libraries began offering Internet access to their customers. This has remained a key service of libraries even now, especially for those customers who do not have a computer at home, do not have Internet access at home, or may need assistance in using the computer or finding information on the Internet. For anyone who has ever relied on the Internet for access to information, e-mail, work, or even entertainment, if that access becomes unavailable for any reason, it can seem like one's life is over. Suddenly that connection to the rest of the world is cut, and it can be a very frightening feeling. (What did we ever do before the Internet?)

For this connection to the Internet to work, all libraries (all networks for that matter) must have a device called a firewall. On a network, this is typically a piece of hardware that sits between the Internet and your network. It has an extremely important job: to manage the traffic that goes from your library's computers out to the Internet and the traffic that comes from the Internet in to your library's computers. Without a properly configured firewall, your network would become the victim of many Internet "attacks" such that the computers on your network would no longer be usable. The firewall acts as the gatekeeper, allowing the good information in and keeping the harmful information out.

NETWORK MANAGEMENT

If all the computers are connected properly, there are software tools available that can help manage the computer network. For example, many libraries have computers running the Windows operating system. In addition, there are usually servers installed with the Windows operating system that can communicate with all the computers on the network to ensure that they are functioning properly and communicating with one another. For example, each computer on the network must have an "address" for it to communicate with the other computers. One role of a server can be to give out the addresses to the computers on the network and make sure they are working.

At the Rochester Hills Public Library, I knew that the antivirus software was not working properly, because the computers on the network did not have updated antivirus software. Another role of a server on a network can be to manage the antivirus software for the computers on the network. Software can be configured to run on a server that regularly downloads updated antivirus software and pushes the updates out to all the computers that need the update. When I discovered computers with outdated antivirus software, I tracked back to the server and found that the computers were not communicating with the antivirus software on the server. There was a breakdown in the network communication.

The network was not entirely broken, as the computers were still able to access the Internet and share some information. However, a properly configured network should definitely have servers that are able to keep the antivirus software up-to-date on all the computers. Sometimes that means that the software for antivirus is not set up correctly. However, in this case, I learned that it was a bigger problem with the computers not being able to send the right information back to the servers on the network. The underlying Windows server software and its management tools had to be reconfigured to send and receive the proper information with the computers on the network. Therefore, this network needed to be corrected for other applications to work properly.

NETWORK SECURITY AND PRIVACY

Libraries have a long history of protecting the privacy of its users. Libraries are public buildings, open to anyone. The Library Privacy Act ensures that libraries will not share the activity of a patron with anyone else. Libraries fight to protect the First Amendment rights of all Americans and do not judge or censor the information that is available. In recent years, with the explosion of the Internet, libraries have been challenged to protect minors from accessing inappropriate information on the Internet in various ways. However, many libraries emphasize that the ultimate responsibility for minors is with their parents. Nonetheless, libraries have a unique responsibility to safely and securely provide access to information for all its patrons.

While computer networks allow access to systems, they must provide security so that access is granted to only those people who need it. Technology security is essential on any network. It is particularly challenging in a library because we allow people to use our technology, but we do not want them to access private library data, such as patron records or financial systems. Therefore, many libraries have a network configuration that separates a staff network from a public network.

First, the usual security on a computer network requires setting permissions so that only authorized users can access the information they need. At a library, this means allowing the library staff to have access to the information they need in order to do their jobs without compromising the private nature of other information. For example, at the Rochester Hills Public Library, there is a Windows network, and each staff member has a username and password that he or she must use to log-in to the computer. This username and password are what enable the staff member to access the resources he or she needs.

In addition, there are folders set up on a server such that staff members have places to save shared resources that can be viewed by their colleagues, as well as individual resources that only one staff member can access. In this way, staff members have some level of privacy, as well as the ability to easily share information with one another. There are also folders where shared information is shared by only a few staff members, such as financial information. This information is highly critical and must be kept safe, but two or three administrative staff might need access to it.

The security described here is common on almost any network where multiple people need to access secure information. However, the extra step in a library is that all of the information accessed by the staff must be kept protected and safe from any of the public users that access public information on the network. This is why a library network should be configured to separate staff and public data on the network. With this properly configured, the public can use the library's network to access the Internet or even library resources, such as the online catalog, website, or subscription databases. But even from a library computer, the users would not be able to gain access to private patron data.

WIRELESS

A wireless network can extend your wired network for mobile devices, but it has unique security considerations as well. In a library, you may want to allow wireless access for both your public users and your staff. Managing wireless access for your public users may require some additional security and policies. For example, will you secure the wireless network with encryption, such as WEP or WPA? If so, you will have to provide a key (or password) to the users for them to connect to the network. Perhaps you will want your public users to log-in with their library card number. If so, you will need some software that can interface with your patron database, perhaps using SIP, which is the main protocol that systems can use to interface with library patron databases. Perhaps you want to keep your wireless network open, in which case anyone can use it.

At the Rochester Hills Public Library, we kept the network open to anyone. However, we did want to have some management of the network. Therefore, we used a gateway for the entry point onto the wireless network, which is a hardware device. In the software for the gateway, we could track how many users would log-in to the wireless network each day by redirecting all users to a generic log-in page. We could also set parameters for the wireless network, such as the hours it was available (only during library hours) and what type of traffic would be allowed on the wireless network. We wanted to limit the traffic so that services would not run and take up all the bandwidth. There-fore, we limited users only to ports that we knew were safe, such as general web traffic and e-mail traffic. In this way, we were able to provide convenient wireless access to our users while still maintaining control over the security of the network.

In addition, you may want to create a way for your staff users to take ad-vantage of the wireless network. In this case, you may want to secure the staff wireless network further, perhaps with a WPA key. Since you likely have control over the devices that you will allow on the staff side of the wireless network, you can configure them with the WPA key, and this will encrypt the data traveling on the staff wireless network.

Finally, for all of this to work, you need wireless access points throughout the library building. Be sure to have enough access points so that anyone from anywhere in the building will be able to pick up a wireless signal. If you have multiple floors in the building, you will likely be better off placing access points on each floor. There are tools available to help lay out a wire-less network for full coverage; many companies can also assist with this. A good wireless network not only provides access for your patrons on their own devices but also allows your staff to roam through the library and maintain access on a portable device, which therefore improves the staff's ability to provide good customer service throughout the building.

SERVERS

In a library, servers are used to help manage the Windows operating system, to store files, to manage the antivirus software, and to maintain the ILS.

Servers act as a central point of communication for many of the computers in the library. If a server is unavailable, likely something on some of the computers will not work properly. Therefore, the next thing that I did at the Rochester Hills Public Library was to review the servers.

Unfortunately, much of the server hardware itself was very old. In general, servers do last longer than client computers—usually 5 or 6 years, if they were purchased initially with enough power and memory for growth. The servers at RHPL were too old and too small to properly support the technology infrastructure for the library. Sometimes, older servers can be used for secondary or less significant functions, as long as newer servers are in place for the primary, most critical roles. In addition, one server can usually run multiple applications, as long as there are enough resources available. Initially, I replaced a few of the most critical servers and then, slowly over time, was able to migrate more of them as time and budget allowed.

INTEGRATED LIBRARY SYSTEM

For most libraries, the ILS is the most important computer system. It tracks the materials in the library as well as all the library users. Anyone who has worked in a library can probably agree that if access to the ILS is unavailable for any reason, most of the work in the library comes to a halt. Librarians are challenged to use their skills learned in library school to help customers find information, and staff usually use some sort of manual or offline method to check items out to customers. The work is considerably more challenging.

One reason that access to the ILS could be unavailable is due to some sort of network interruption, as discussed. The other reason is due to a problem with the server running the ILS itself. This is why it is very important to select a system that fits well with your library's needs and to have a good partnership with your system's vendor. Your library's relationship with your system's vendor is never more important than when your system is down and you need assistance.

One of my first projects at the Rochester Hills Public Library was to migrate the library to the Polaris ILS. I was grateful on many occasions that we had such a good partnership with Polaris, as it was always responsive to problems that came up and helpful in resolving issues in a timely fashion. Furthermore, our initial migration to the Polaris ILS went very smoothly. We spent time working through the planning and configuring of the system together—staff from Polaris and staff from the library were involved every step of the way to ensure that the result would meet everyone's expectations.

In addition, the actual configuration of the system and the features that are made available can make or break your ILS. A good ILS will have a number of features that can streamline the work of the staff and provide quality information to the public users. Depending on your community, one may be more important than the other, but I argue that both work together to create a successful ILS experience. I have seen on many occasions where staff members would be frustrated with the ILS because it "cannot" do something they need. Upon further investigation, it can. The feature either needs to be configured, or the permissions to do it need to be changed, or perhaps an upgrade of the system is needed—but it can be done. An ILS is a complicated system, which is again why the relationship with your vendor is so important.

TEAMWORK

No matter what technology project you are doing in your library, involve staff as early on in the process as you can. I cannot emphasize that enough. When you create a project team, include front-line staff and decision makers. The ultimate goal is to end up with a system that best meets your library's needs and the needs of your library users. Working with staff who are involved with the system every day is the best way to accomplish this. In addition to the staff at your library, partner with the vendor that is providing the system. You are the expert about your library, and the vendor is the expert about the system. Working together, you will be able to implement a system of any kind that works well in your library.

When implementing a new system, communication is also extremely important. This includes letting the staff know how the project is going, what the time frame is, and what they can expect to happen next. In addition, it is essential to include staff training in the project. They will be interacting with the system on a daily basis and using it to interact with patrons. The more they know, the better customer service they will be able to provide to the community.

It is also important to let patrons know what they should expect as changes unfold. If the system will be down, let them know using announcements on your website, newsletter, or local newspaper. If your staff are still learning the new system, patrons will likely be more patient if you post small signs at public service desks explaining the situation. In the end, share relevant information as much as you can, and everyone involved will be better equipped to handle the experience.

PUBLIC COMPUTERS AND SYSTEMS

Public computers in libraries are generally available for anyone to come in and use. Therefore, managing them requires some extra care to keep them running and reliable. Public computers likely will have to be upgraded approximately every 4 years, as budget allows. The software on them will be upgraded more frequently. Libraries find management tools that can "image" computers helpful so that information technology staff can set up one computer and then image or copy the setup to many other computers. In addition, software such as Deep Freeze is available so that any changes made on the computer by a public user are lost when the computer is restarted.

Software systems are available that manage how users must sign up to use a computer and how long their session can be. Also, the systems can manage any printing done and charge appropriate fees. All of these systems and more can help a library with the logistics of providing computers with Internet access to the public. The better these systems work, the less the public service staff will have to worry about any problems, so they will be free to provide the best help to the patrons.

VIRTUALIZATION

After a few years when the network, servers, computers, and systems were stable and robust, I started investigating the use of virtualization. This is a technology that allows two or three very powerful servers to run multiple "virtual" servers. In addition, using a storage area network to hold all the data, instead of putting them on multiple servers, increases the speed and reliability of the data. In the end, a virtual environment can save a great deal of money (less hardware to maintain, less power to run the hardware, less heat created by the hardware) and make the management of the infrastructure easier.

The Rochester Hills Public Library has a virtual network created with VM-Ware software. Approximately 15 virtual servers are running on 3 physical servers. And the possibilities are practically endless.

CONCLUSION

Take technology projects one at a time, prioritizing those that have the biggest impact on the library. New technology makes it much easier for your staff members to do their jobs. Good technology services enable your patrons to easily access what they need and experience how your library can enrich their lives. Whether your library has a dynamic website and online catalog, self-checkout machines, a state-of-the-art computer lab, or optimal access for mobile users, there is something for everyone. Build a solid foundation, and you will have the infrastructure in place on which to grow.

For more information on the details on the project implementation process, check out my book *Implementing Technology Solutions in Libraries*, with some resources on my website, http://www.karencknox.com/itsil.

3

The Darien Library's Picture Book Reorganization: A Collection Designed with Patrons in Mind

Kiera Parrott

The Darien Library

On January 10, 2009, the new Darien Library in southeastern Connecticut opened its doors to some 7,200 eager patrons. The library had been closed for 6 weeks, and during that time, it moved from a small and overcrowded building on Leroy Avenue, where it had been for over 50 years, to a 54,000-square-foot, state-of-the-art, LEED-certified facility located just a stone's throw away down Post Road. When children and parents streamed into the new Children's Library, they found more than brand new furniture, a toddler play space, and a dedicated technology lab for children. They walked into a children's library in which the collection had been redesigned and re-organized with the needs of children and their caregivers in mind, a collection that abandoned the old ways of picture book cataloging and instead placed the experience of the users squarely at the center of the design.

FORESTS AND GLADES

The decision to reorganize the picture book and early learning materials began several months before the move from the old Darien Library to the new building. It was inspired by the work being done to reorganize the adult nonfiction collection. The adult services librarians had been brainstorming ways to make their large collection of nonfiction materials more accessible and browsable for patrons. They described the nonfiction collection as a "forest of shelves," in which patrons could easily become overwhelmed. The idea was to create "glades" within that forest: areas in which subjects were called out and highlighted. Instead of creating a dark, forbidding forest of materials, they sought to organize the collection into smaller, more inviting sections.

The adult services librarians came up with nine sections that became known as "the glades." These included Lives, Times, Play, Work, Nature, Body and Soul, Places, Art, and Literature. This new system of glades lie atop the traditional Dewey decimal classification system, thereby achieving the goal of creating smaller, more browsable sections while maintaining searchability and findability. The Children's Library staff were impressed.

The children's librarians began thinking about their own collection of materials. Was there a way to reorganize into "glades" that would make the children's collection easier to navigate for children, parents, and caregivers? One type of children's literature immediately came to mind: picture books. Picture books are illustrated books that use words and illustrations to communicate. Unlike most other formats within a children's library, picture books span a wide age range and an almost limitless variety of subjects. There are picture books for learning about colors and shapes, picture books explaining death to children, picture books that rhyme, picture books that retell classic folklore. In the traditional classification scheme, these books are lumped together and shelved alphabetically by the author's last name. There are also illustrated nonfiction picture books that are often shelved in Dewey decimal order. These books generally live in sections used primarily by older elementary children. For years the children's librarians had observed patrons wander through the picture book collection, trying to find a book appropriate for their child. Patrons would often ask the librarians the following kinds of questions:

"My child is two and loves truck books. Where is your truck section?"
"My daughter likes reading about animals. She's in preschool. Where is that section?"
"We love the books you choose for storytime. Is there a section of those books?"

Under the old classification schema, the answers to all three questions are complicated. There is no truck section for toddlers, no animal section for preschoolers, and no storytime collection. But could there be? The librarians observed two common traits among patrons in the children's library:

- The majority of parents and caregivers using the picture book collection select books for prereaders (generally, children aged 5 years and under).
- The criteria for picture book selection most often involved a child's age or developmental level and an area of interest.

Parents and caregivers had to use the catalog or consult a librarian for assistance. Should they simply wish to browse, which was most often what these patrons desired, the arrangement of the picture books proved challenging to navigate. The traditional alphabetic arrangement was not designed with the needs of browsers in mind. Was the old system the best way to meet the needs of these patrons? Could there be a better organization that would allow for findability and a satisfying browsing experience?

The Children's Library staff immediately set to work brainstorming ways in which the picture book collection could be reorganized to better suit the needs of its primary users. The overall goal was to create a collection that would easy and pleasurable for patrons to use. Patrons searching for specific titles or authors should be able to find what they wanted with ease; parents and care-givers looking for developmentally appropriate and fun read-alouds for their prereaders should enjoy browsing the collection; children who could not yet read or identify letters should be able to discover books for themselves. The time frame was tight; the project would need to be planned and executed in less than 4 months, 6 weeks of which would be during a period when the library was closed to the public. The goal was to launch the new organization simultane-ously with the opening of the new library building on January 10, 2009.

PICTURE BOOK GLADES AND THE BIRTH OF THE FIRST FIVE YEARS COLLECTION

Early stages in the picture book reorganization involved many conversations among the staff about how patrons used and accessed the current collection, how the physical layout of the new building would affect shelving options, and what kinds of sections could and should make up the new picture book area. Using free online software called FreeMind, which allowed the librar-ians to create a mind map (Figure 3.1), the librarians created several visual representations of their proposed picture book groupings. It proved to be a great way to organize and archive somewhat disorganized and free-flowing ideas that were emerging at a fast pace.

The mind maps went through several iterations and revisions during the discussions. Some sections were obvious to the staff: folk and fairy tales, picture books about nature and animals, award winners, transportation. Oth-ers were more esoteric and took time to define: books about developmental milestones, books about emotions and phobias, conceptual books.

Throughout this process of defining picture book glades, it became appar-ent to the staff that this new collection would comprise more than just picture books. The librarians thought carefully about the primary user group for this collection: prereaders and their caregivers. Prereaders are children who are not reading independently and who encounter books mostly through a shared reading experience with an adult. Prereaders are also emerging readers. They are starting to identify letters, letter sounds, words, and simple sentences.

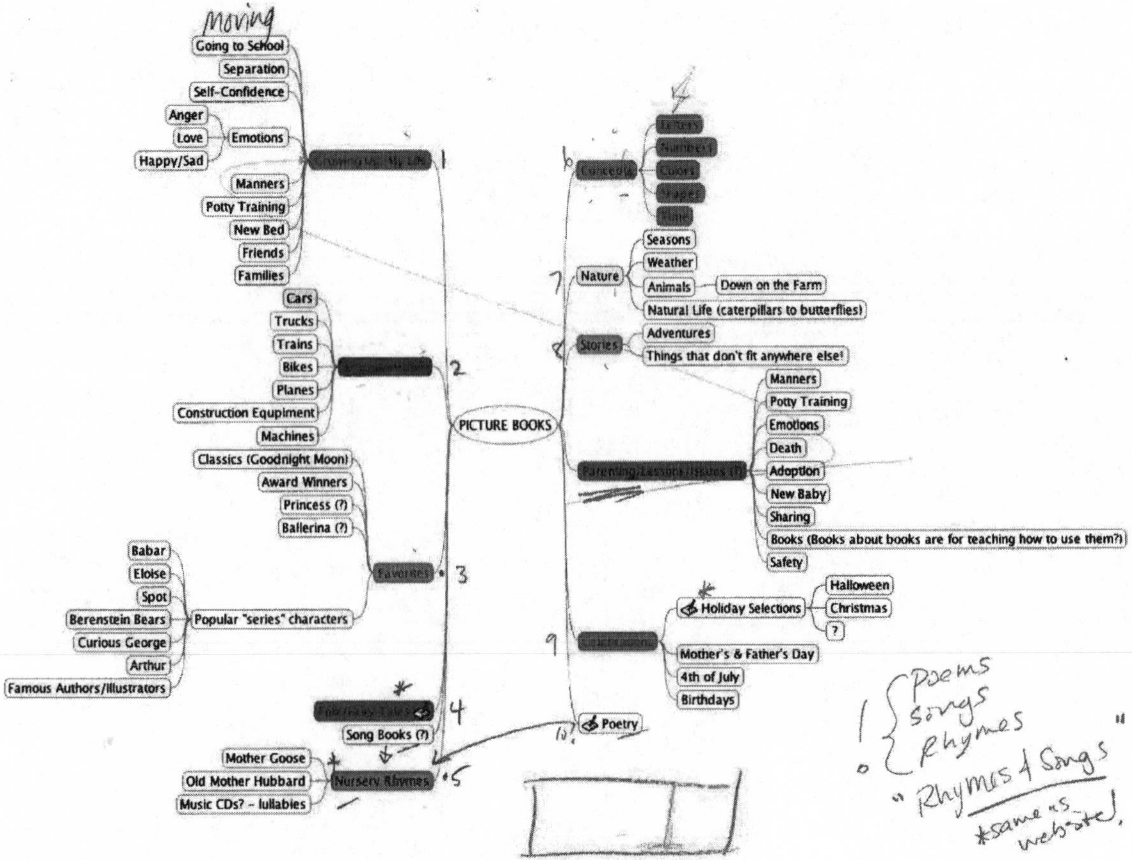

Figure 3.1. The mind map used to brainstorm sections in the First Five Years collection.

Since all prereaders are also emerging readers, it was important to create a collection that encompassed that wide range of development. The librarians considered the literature on early literacy and how children acquire preliteracy skills during their first 5 years of life. They wanted to create a collection that would span the reading and literacy-building needs of a child from babyhood through his or her emergence as a new reader. The First Five Years collection was born.

The newly imagined First Five Years collection would include board books (durable cardboard books intended for infants), picture books, easy readers (also known as beginning chapter books), and multimedia (e.g., audio books, book-with-CD kits, CD-ROM games, and DVDs) all geared for ages 5 years and younger. Since this new collection would serve the needs of prereaders as well as their caregivers, the reorganized collection would include materials on parenting topics. After much discourse and fine-tuning, the final list of sections that would live within the First Five Years collection was created (Table 3.1).

During this time, it was decided that the sections would be color coordinated. This would help patrons navigate the collection visually, help define the sections in the new physical arrangement of shelves, and, perhaps most important, allow prereaders to browse more easily. By identifying the new sections by color, even children who could not yet read would be able to see where one section ended and another began. They would also be able to identify their favorite parts of the collection. The color would be indicated on the spine label and on signage.

Discussion of spine labels and signage also lead to decisions on how these new picture book glades would be described in the online catalog. All of the materials in the First Five Years collection would be identified by the prefix F5, followed by the name of the glade and the bibliographic information (typically, the author's last name or a Dewey classification number). For example, a picture book in the Nature section of the First Five Years collection written by John Smith would have the call number "F5 Nature SMITH." The call number of each book corresponded to the shelf location, thereby providing a simple address for patrons searching for specific titles (Table 3.2).

REORGANIZING 16,000 BOOKS IN 6 WEEKS

Once the glades were decided, it was time to begin reorganizing the existing picture book, board book, and easy reader collections into the new sections. This was a several-step process:

- First, the existing books had to be evaluated one by one and given a new designation.

Table 3.1.   The Final List of Selections within the First Five Years Collection

Glade Name	Description
Favorites	Classic authors and illustrators of picture books for children up to age 5, Caldecott winners, ultrapopular series picture books
Nature	Nonanthropomorphized animal stories, seasons, earth, natural cycles, environment
Folk and Fairy Tales	Fairy tales and folk tales for children up to age 5
Concepts	The alphabet, numbers, colors, opposites, shapes, and other simple concepts
Transportation	Cars, trucks, planes, construction equipment, and other things that go
Rhymes and Songs	Books in rhyme, books based on a song, nursery rhymes, Mother Goose tales
Growing Up	Milestones such as the first day of school and losing first tooth, books about sibling relationships, family relations, manners, emotions
Celebrations	Valentine's Day, Easter, St. Patrick's Day, Halloween, Christmas, Jewish holidays, all other observed holidays, stories about world festivals, birthday stories, wedding stories
Stories	Picture books that do not fit neatly into any of the categories (many of the bedtime stories and fantasy stories live in this section)
Learn to Read	This section contains beginning chapter books, also known as easy readers, designed to help brand new readers learn sight words, increase vocabulary, and improve comprehension. Popular books in this section include the Henry and Mudge series by Cynthia Rylant and the Fly Guy books by Ted Arnold
Parents	Parenting advice and guidance, as well as issue-based picture books explaining, for example, sexuality and puberty, death and grieving, special needs, potty training, new baby, adoption, divorce, stranger danger
Board Books	Sturdy board books for infants

- Next, the book would be retrofitted with the new spine labels and an RFID tag (standard on all materials in the new Darien Library).
- Then, the MARC record for each book would need to be updated to reflect the new collection code and call number.
- Finally, after all of the above was completed, the books would need to be packed and moved to the new building, where they would be shelved along with their new counterparts in the First Five Years collection.

The most staff-intensive part of the process was evaluating the existing collection and determining which new glade each book would move into under

Table 3.2.   Spine Labels and Signage of the New Picture Book Glades

First Five Years Collection	Call Number	Color Spine Label
Favorites	F5 Faves	Pink
Nature	F5 Nature	Green
Folk and Fairy Tales	F5 Ftales	White
Concepts	F5 Concepts	Purple
Transportation	F5 Transport	Red
Rhymes and Songs	F5 Rhymes	Dark blue
Growing Up	F5 Growing	Light blue
Celebrations	F5 Celebrate	Orange
Stories	F5 Stories	Yellow
Learn to Read	F5 Learn	Light blue
Parents	F5 Parents	Clear
Board Books	F5 Board	No spine label

the new system. At this time, the staff were working in the old building. The process began approximately 1 month before the closing of the building to the public. Small sections of the children's library were taped off while staff worked on evaluating each item. Once the building was closed to the public, the librarians were able to designate whole sections of the room for various collections. As each staff member evaluated a book and determined which new section to place it, he or she would then bring that book over to a corner or area marked for similar items. Once there were enough books gathered, another staff member would begin the process of applying the retrofitted labels. Finally, the retrofitted books would be placed on a cart and sent to another staff member, who would update the MARC records.

Librarians could be heard shouting from one corner of the library to the other, asking for a second or third opinion on which section a book should go. Sometimes if a particular book proved challenging, an impromptu meeting was called, and a small gathering of children's library staff members would look at the book in question, debate various options, and pronounce judgment. In the end, over 16,000 children's books were individually evaluated and relabeled by a staff member over the course of 6 weeks. It took a staff of four full-time librarians and about five part-time library assistants to accomplish this ambitious task in the given time frame.

THE DEBUT

A few days before the grand opening of the new building, local reporters and bloggers were invited for a sneak preview of the new Darien Library. One

local mom and avid blogger summed up her experience of the children's
library:

> What impressed me most about the new Darien Library is the fact that the
> books, everywhere, but especially in the children's room, have been shelved,
> labeled and organized in a way that makes me feel less like a moron and more
> empowered to find what I'm looking for on my own. . . . The reason this speaks
> to me, in addition to the fact that it's relieving me of the need to curse myself
> for not paying closer attention to card-cataloging techniques in middle school, is
> because I feel like the Library, which in my mind used to be a little intimidating
> and kind of like a disapproving Mother, is reaching out to ME.[1]

Like Ms. Lyons, parents, caregivers, and children using the newly reorganized collection were discovering great titles, encountering developmentally
appropriate materials, and finding it easier to browse for books. A few weeks
after the grand opening on January 10, 2009, a young boy under 3 years old
was overheard shouting to his grandfather, "Look, look! Let me show you my
section. It's the red books because I love truck books." This young prereader
was able to identify and share his favorite kind of books by simply knowing
the color-coordinated section of the library. Success!

ASSESSMENT: COMPARING CIRCULATION STATISTICS

The librarians suspected that patrons were using the First Five Years collection more than they had used the old picture book collection. There was
anecdotal evidence and overheard conversations that led the staff to believe
that the reorganization was a resounding success. Now, the job was to find
out exactly how much of a success.

Prior to the reorganization, the picture books and easy readers in fiscal year
2007–2008 had circulated a total of 18,926 times. After the move to the new
building and the debut of the reorganized First Five Years collection, the circulation increased to 50,298—an increase of over 165%. The following year
saw an even more dramatic jump. The First Five Years collection circulated
a total of 81,224 times, representing a percentage increase of over 300% from
2008. Before the reorganization, children's materials constituted 33.5% of the
entire Darien Library circulation. After the reorganization, children's books
represent 41.4% of Darien Library's entire circulation. It was clear: Patrons
were utilizing the reorganized collection much more than they had in the past.
Four years after the opening of the new Darien Library, the circulation of
the children's collection remains strong, averaging over 40% of the library's
entire circulation per year.

Fine-tuning of each glade within the First Five Years collection continues. As new books are acquired and older books wax and wane in popularity, the librarians are continually evaluating each section and determining which titles are most appropriate. Books tend to move in and out of various glades. It is a living collection that grows and changes as the needs of its community of users changes. The guiding criteria for each cataloging decision stems from one essential question: Where would a patron most likely look for this item? If the answer to that question is contrary to traditional cataloging methods, it is placed in the new section nonetheless. The ease of findability for the users of the children's library is always the most important factor.

NEXT STEPS

As new formats arise, they have been integrated into the First Five Years collection. Most recent acquisitions have included circulating Early Literacy iPad Kits and a mounted iPad preloaded with apps and interactive e-books for young children. These devices allow children and parents in the First Five Years collection to experience a new technology and discover age-appropriate apps for their children.

The reorganization that created the First Five Years collection also produced the Kids collection. This collection contains materials for children reading independently and includes more sophisticated picture books for older readers, chapter books (also known as transitional books), middle grade fiction, nonfiction, biographies, and graphic novels. Aside from the fact that it abandons the antiquated term "juvenile" in favor of the more friendly and colloquial "kids," this collection is fairly traditional in arrangement. The children's library staff has been looking closely at the Kids nonfiction section in particular and musing about possible ways to make it more accessible and easier to browse. Several libraries, most of them school libraries, have begun to ditch the Dewey decimal classification system in favor of creating nonfiction collections for children that are more intuitive. The children's librarians at Darien Library are currently gathering information on these Dewey-less transformations. Whether the Kids nonfiction section abandons Dewey altogether or simply applies a browsing-friendly layer modeled after the adult nonfiction collections has yet to be determined.

ADVICE

After the opening of the new Darien Library in 2009, many libraries came for tours and visits. As a result, several libraries have since adopted the "Darien model" for picture book reorganization. Since each community is unique and the needs of the library users are slightly different at each library, most libraries reorganizing their picture book collections have adapted the model to suit their community of users. For example, libraries with a large collection of princess stories and high demand for those materials have created entire "Princess" sections.

Before undertaking a reorganization of any collection, take a survey of existing materials and the users. Begin by looking at the collection and determining the strengths. Does your picture book collection have a phenomenal assortment of folktales? How do patrons most often ask for and discover those titles? Perhaps it might be useful to organize them by region rather than by author or title. Take a survey of your users. Find out what kinds of materials and topics they most often look for in the library and how they search. The goal should be making that process as simply and enjoyable as possible.

Finally, plan for revisions. In the course of dividing up an existing picture book collection into 12 new sections, we made plenty of wrong decisions. Some books that wound up in F5 Growing needed to be changed to F5 Nature. Whole sections of F5 Favorites eventually got moved to F5 Stories. Having staff understand that the new collection was a work in progress and having a process in place for continually evaluating titles and making necessary changes helped define and fine-tune the glades.

Reorganizing a collection is a big commitment. Not only must existing items be retrofitted and recataloged, but new acquisitions must also meet the updated standards. Whether processing happens in-house or via a vendor, it's important to have the entire staff on board with the decision. The benefits are worth the up-front commitment in time and resources: picture book circulation will increase dramatically; staff will have a deeper understanding of the collection; and most important, patrons will have a markedly better experience using the collection.

NOTE

1. Nicole Lyons, *All about Darien Blog*, January 7, 2009, http://www.dariendotmom.com/blog/local_dotmom/arounddarien/kids/the-new-darien-library-its-for-me/.

4

STARS: Launching a Customer Service Model in Riverside County

MARK SMITH
The Riverside County Library

Did you ever hear the quote attributed to Margaret Mead that says, "Never doubt that a small group of thoughtful, committed citizens can change the world. Indeed, it is the only thing that ever has"? That observation comes to mind when I remember the experience of the Riverside County Library System (RCLS) in June 2005 when the management team and five staff members met to consider recommendations for how to revitalize our approach to customer service. This exercise—which began as a task to create a program for our annual staff development day (All Staff Day)—blossomed into a full-blown, systemwide customer service program called STARS. In the following years, STARS had a profound and lasting impact on library service in not only the RCLS but a number of libraries across the United States.

BACKGROUND

At more than 7,400 square miles, Riverside County is one of the largest counties in the United States and stretches from a border with Los Angeles, Orange, and San Diego counties in the west to the Arizona border in the east. Located in the Inland Empire region of Southern California, much of the county is desert, and all of it is a dry climate that typically receives less than 2 inches of rain per year. The RCLS service area includes approximately 1.1 million persons.

From its establishment as a county library in 1911 until 1997, the Riverside County Library was operated by the City of Riverside as a joint city-county library. For a variety of reasons, in 1997 Riverside County decided to sever its 85-year arrangement with the City of Riverside and begin running its own library. The county sought bids to operate the library, and the winning proposal was from Library Systems & Services (LSSI), a library management and support company from Germantown, Maryland. On July 1, 1997, RCLS became the first library in the United States to be managed on a daily basis by employees of a private company. Beginning in July 1997, Riverside County, in partnership with LSSI, began to invest in a series of long-overdue upgrades to the county library system's services and physical infrastructure. These improvements included increasing the number of hours the system was open (which more than doubled in the first 5 years of operation); renovating, replacing, or adding facilities (the system has grown from 25 libraries in 1997 to 33 in 2012, with nearly 200,000 additional square feet); and adding key programs, such as English as a second language, a robust Latino outreach program, an early literacy program, and a strong emphasis on adult programming.

By 2005, the public had seen many significant improvements in the quality of services, collections, facilities, and programming in the Riverside County Library. With a sense that key infrastructural elements had been addressed, the LSSI/RCLS management team—consisting of the library administrator, deputy administrator, regional managers, and automation manager—began considering a more concerted approach to customer service improvements. While library management had always stressed the importance of customer service, what had been lacking was a systematic approach to changing the organizational culture to put the customer first and a recognition of how such issues as staff morale, training, and documentation could affect customer service.

GETTING STARTED

Motivated by these concerns, in May 2005, the RCLS/LSSI management team selected five RCLS employees to form a work team to consider several issues pertaining to customer service. The employees chosen represented different parts of the county and different sizes of libraries and included four branch managers and one paraprofessional staff member. The individuals were Tracie Carignan, manager of the large Glen Avon Library in the far western side of the county; Jeannie Kays, manager of the large Palm Desert Library, a facility colocated with the College of the Desert Library in the Coachella Valley region in the eastern part of the county; Connie Rynning, manager of the smaller Woodcrest branch in the suburban area near the City of Riverside; Jan Kuebel, manager of the Home Gardens Library serving a largely Latino community between the cities of Riverside and Corona; and

Angelica Trummel, a children's services associate at the Grace Mellman Library, a midsized library serving the relatively affluent community of Temecula in Southwestern Riverside County.

The first meeting of the work team presented the following questions:

- How could the RCLS take a comprehensive approach to ensuring consistently high customer service?
- What are the key elements needed to create a customer-focused organizational culture?
- Can we identify industry best practices that we should use as a model?

As though this assignment could be any more challenging, the management team asked the work team if it could produce its results in time to present a program at the annual staff development day known as All Staff Day, set for the end of July. That gave the group barely 2 months to research the questions posed, develop recommendations, and present its findings to the full library staff.

The work team members never hesitated. They immediately accepted the challenge and began their research with great energy and determination. The team began the process with a good amount of discussion and research. They consulted a variety of online resources both within and outside the library profession. They looked at a variety of customer service models, including the FISH model (Lundin & Christensen, 2000), Disney's customer service training model, the Nordstrom model (Spector & McCarthy, 2005), and the Malcolm Baldridge Performance Excellence Program (National Institute of Standards and Technology, 2012). They considered the National Retail Federation's (2012) customer service certification program. They visited many libraries online to see who had developed customer service models.

In the course of their research, the team discovered that the Cerritos Library, about 50 miles away in Los Angeles County, had developed an internal customer service model called "Wow Service." This library, then under the direction of director Waynn Pearson, has received many accolades for its unique building, which features a shark tank, a full *Tyrannosaurus rex* skeleton, and many other marvels, along with many new approaches to providing excellent customer service. The RCLS team contacted the library and spoke to Jackie Stetson, the library's operations supervisor, who administered the customer service plan. The Cerritos model had several aspects that the team appreciated and felt would work well. Cerritos staff were trained to consider library patrons as "guests," and they were encouraged to learn their names. Staff were encouraged to get out from behind public service desks and move around the library actively asking the public if it needed help. All employees were given name badges (first names only), and some were outfitted with headsets to aide their ability to provide quick and accurate service. RCLS staff learned a new term from the Cerritos staff: "emotional leakage," meaning the tendency to allow personal problems to show while at work, something very much discouraged at Cerritos. While RCLS gathered positive examples from other libraries and organizations, the Cerritos "Wow Service" model came the closest to the total, integrated approach that the team had in mind.

STARS IS BORN

After gathering this information, the team came back together to discuss its findings. The members of the team found themselves in agreement on several points:

- RCLS was ready for a comprehensive customer service plan that would introduce key concepts to staff and would integrate with all aspects of the operation.
- Staff needed to be trained in several key elements of service.
- Ways should be found to solicit customer feedback.
- Staff morale is a key component in customer service; consequently, staff opinion on library procedures should be sought and a means found to recognize and honor employees who provide exemplary service.
- Communication is key to motivating staff and helps to ensure more consistent application of policies and procedures.

The team discussed a variety of ideas for early projects that would support each point, including comment cards, staff rewards, training programs, and more clarity regarding policies and procedures.

What was lacking, however, was a name for the program. I held up one hand with fingers outstretched and challenged the committee to name and program with five easy-to-remember points. Another committee member said, "With five points, like a star." At once, the committee began ticking off the points of the star that would form the acronym:

S—Smile: Create a welcome environment in the library.
T—Ten-foot rule: Meaning, to speak to anyone within 10 feet.
A—Attitude: Emphasizing that working in a library should be fun.
R—Response: Listening for customer feedback.
S—Satisfaction: Did the customer get what she or he came for?

And thus, STARS was born, and the committee had a structure not only for its recommendations to library management but also to go forth and build a program for All Staff Day. (Subsequently, the *T* in STARS became "Talk to 'em" because the committee learned that the 10-foot rule is a patented training motto of a major U.S. retail chain.)

With the enthusiastic encouragement of the RCLS management team, the STARS team began planning a full set of recommendations and its program for All Staff Day. The program became a labor of love for the committee. It developed a set of skits to illustrate each of the five points of the program. The STARS team worked fast, and by the time of All Staff Day in July 2005, it was ready to present.

All Staff Day at that point had been presented for 5 previous years, and a format had been developed and used in each preceding year, which involved an opening session with three sets of breakouts. In 2005, however, the debut of the STARS program demanded a different model. The All Staff Day planning committee opted for one long general session in the morning to give proper time for the introduction of the STARS program. The keynote speaker for All Staff Day that year was Ron Dubberly, former director of the Seattle Public Library and Atlanta Public Library and a president of the Public Library Association (Dubberly had also served as the first administrator of the RCLS for 9 months in 1997 while a permanent administrator was sought, and he later became the CEO of LSSI). Dubberly's topic was customer service and the various models that exist, including the Nordstrom model and others.

Dubberly's keynote address was immediately followed by an introduction of STARS by the members of the committee. Addressing the nearly 300 LSSI employees of the RCLS, the team discussed its charge, research, and findings. The team introduced the concept of the five points of STARS and then began its skits, which were presented with great hilarity. Illustrating the ten-foot rule, the group had an actual 10-foot ruler as a prop. In another skit, the concept of emotional baggage was represented as an actual trunk full of problems that an employee carried throughout her workday in the library. The audience watched as the STARS team depicted frustrated customers waiting for employees to conclude lengthy personal (and embarrassing!) conversations at the service desk, among other public service disasters.

Following the skits, the audience was highly upbeat and engaged in a conversation about the nature of the STARS program and how the staff saw it developing as a tool to achieve better service in the RCLS. The staff seemed all the more motivated to make STARS work because it was a program developed by staff members and not imposed from above by the management team.

THE STARS RECOMMENDATIONS

After the auspicious debut of STARS at the 2005 LSSI/RCLS All Staff Day, the STARS team went to work to refine its set of recommendations for initial activities. The following emerged as the first set of recommended projects for the STARS committee.

Public Feedback

The committee had two immediate recommendations. First was the creation of a comment card. Many examples were gathered from retail establishments, and a particular design was recommended. The adopted design could be folded into a mailer preaddressed to the administrative office, or it could be left off with library staff. This concept was immediately designed by the LSSI graphic artist and printed. (This comment card is still in use and has since been adopted by every other LSSI library on the West Coast.)

The other idea for public feedback was to create clipboards that could be located at the front desk of libraries to collect comments. These clipboards would be bright yellow and have a sign that said, "How are we doing?" Customers would be allowed to write whatever they wanted to on the attached pad, and the results would be collected and returned to the library administrator for review. These clipboards were created and distributed to the library branches, and they collected many interesting comments.

Staff Training and Support

A number of proposals were suggested in this area.

Orientation materials. The STARS team noted the lack of codified documentation to support staff in performing their duties, such as policy and procedures manuals. The policies and procedures manuals that were in use dated back to the 1990s and the Riverside City-County Library System. While there had been periodic updates to the manuals, they had not been codified and were difficult to use, and some procedures were outdated. The STARS team believed that consistent documentation was key to the consistent application of library policy and procedures, which in turn was a key element of quality customer service. This recommendation resulted in two main outcomes. First and most immediate, a staff committee was formed to create a new circulation manual covering such topics as how to make library cards, how to check materials in and out, how to open and close, and much more. The second and longer-term outcome was the complete review and rewrite of the key library policies. Over the next 2 years, LSSI staff, working with the county librarian (a public employee who oversees the LSSI contract), recommended updated policies in circulation, registration, materials collection, the meeting room, foster children, and display. Pending approval of these policies by the Riverside County Board of Supervisors, these policy drafts were included in the new procedures manual.

Identifying pointless or redundant tasks. The STARS team suggested that staff be asked to recommend unneeded and time-wasting tasks for elimination. This project was done, and some tasks were actually eliminated as a result.

Scripts for staff use. The team suggested that staff would find scripts helpful, especially those needed to manage difficult interactions and communicate library policy. Some of these scripts were developed and provided to staff, along with key phrases that help diffuse and manage potentially difficult situations.

Development of training plans. Staff would have comprehensive and individually tailored training plans that would provide for a specific number of training hours per year per employee. Training would include targeted training provided by LSSI as well as attendance at workshops, webinars, conferences, and other outside training opportunities. While some training was added (more on this later), training never reached the level envisioned by the STARS team. Nevertheless, the STARS recommendation did result in a higher level of training than existed before and throughout LSSI, as well as a companywide customer service training plan (more later).

Job sharing and job shadowing. The team recommended that employees be allowed to trade places and work in different branches and to shadow other staff—especially supervisors—to get a feel for what other people in the organization do each day. Some of this occurred, though not to the extent envisioned by the STARS team.

Communications

Intranet and communications from management. An often-heard concern from staff was that they would like to have better ongoing communication from upper management and among staff. The STARS team recommended the creation of a staff Intranet to facilitate information sharing to and among staff. This project was actually already in the planning stage, and the "RCLS Insider" was introduced soon after the Team made its recommendations, though the particular nature of the Intranet was greatly influenced by the STARS team recommendations.

E-mail for all staff. Prior to this time, not all staff had RCLS/LSSI e-mail access. In particular, the page staff did not have e-mail. So that communications could flow more easily to all staff, the STARS team recommended that all staff have e-mail. This was accomplished quickly, and all staff who did not have a desk station were provided access to a computer to be able to check their work e-mail accounts.

Distribution of newsletter to all staff. When all staff had e-mail, they then could receive the LSSEye company newsletter, a recommendation of the STARS team.

All-branch manager meetings. The RCLS is divided into four regions known as "zones." The STARS team recommended that more frequent "All-Zone" meetings be held, to be attended by all branch and regional managers. This was easily accomplished, and meetings have continued to be held at least twice per year ever since, providing yet another avenue for communicating with all staff and ensuring that the same information is conveyed to all managers.

Daily meetings. The STARS team found that a hallmark of quality customer service was frequent staff meetings to communicate current developments and provide an opportunity for staff to share information with one another. The team recommended that branch managers and other supervisors throughout the system be encouraged to hold regular meetings with their staff, preferably on a daily basis. While management encouraged this, it was not a requirement, though zone managers now routinely monitor how frequently branch managers meet with their staffs to ensure that regular communications flows to everyone.

Staff Morale

Recognition for good customer service. The STARS team recommended that a way be found to recognize employees who demonstrate excellent customer service in a specific incident or on an ongoing basis. LSSI already had in place a tiered system of employee recognitions that included instant-reward gift cards, Employee of the Month (and Year) awards, and an annual merit-based performance review. However, the team felt that there should be a separate recognition for a customer service job well done. In response, management introduced star service pins. Upon a recommendation from a supervisor or coworker, an employee would be sent a letter (with a copy inserted into his or her personnel file) from the library administrator, noting one's customer service success, along with a silver star (silver in color only, unfortunately). Upon receipt of four silver stars, the fifth star would be gold. This recognition proved very popular, and many employees wore their stars on their name tags, lanyards, and lapels. This recognition is still in place, and to date, hundreds of stars and letters have been awarded, providing to all staff examples of the type of customer service excellence that is valued and demonstrating that management recognizes when staff provide an extra measure of service.

Group events and activities. The STARS team recommended that activities be held, such as picnics and other events, to gather staff and provide a chance to socialize off work time. LSSI hosts an annual holiday party as well as the annual All Staff Day discussed earlier. However, the STARS team felt that additional social events would be a morale boost. Some events were held soon after this recommendation; however, this particular activity did not take hold as a regular event.

Staff suggestion box. Until this time, there was no regular suggestion box for staff comments, but, following the STARS team recommendations, such a box was set up in the form of an e-mail account that could be used to submit suggestions.

Other suggestions. The STARS team made a number of other suggestions that ranged from providing T-shirts to all staff, improving building security, giving extra help with difficult customer interactions, and offering peer training and mentoring programs. Some of these were implemented, some not, but they provided a roadmap for development for at least 2 years following the initial STARS team recommendations.

STARS AND LIBRARIES GOING FORWARD

STARS turned out to be one of the most ambitious and productive projects of the last 15 years in the RCLS. The program yielded many improvements in customer service in the library system and led to a higher level of staff morale, improved communications, and an overall recognition of the importance of customer service. This recognition extended well beyond Riverside County. Recognizing the benefits of STARS in Riverside County, LSSI upper management began contemplating how this customer service improvements could be achieved in all libraries operated by LSSI across the country (currently, there are 18 library jurisdictions under LSSI operation, including 68 facilities in 6 states). To this end, LSSI designated an individual to be the company-wide customer service trainer. This person was a long-time LSSI employee from California, Jemima Perry, a much-beloved colleague who had a winning and inimitable style of training that promulgated the benefits of providing excellent customer service to every employee in the company. Jemima developed a series of workshops that began with Customer Service 101, continued through Managing Difficult Customers, and included Telephone Etiquette and Customer Service for Supervisors. In the course of 3 years, every LSSI employee participated in this series of trainings. Much to the sadness of her coworkers across the country, Jemima Perry died in February 2012, but her legacy of customer service training is now being carried forward by another employee with her own unique style of presentation. Thus, customer service excellence and customer-focused service remains a central priority for LSSI in Riverside County and companywide.

Nevertheless, things change and time moves on, and after a while, the STARS team, which continued for a time after its initial recommendations, eventually ceased to meet, and while many of the recommendations put in place in 2005 and 2006 remain in effect, many new employees have come on board since then who do not know what the STARS program was.

But that may be changing. Last year, sensing the need to have a staff group that looks at the big picture and makes recommendations for improvement, a group of energetic and creative RCLS/LSSI library staff got together to form a staff committee called Libraries Going Forward. This group met several times in 2011 and 2012 and developed a series of recommendations to send to the RCLS management team. Just as the 2005 All Staff Day hinged on recommendations of the STARS team, the 2012 All Staff Day theme was "Libraries Going Forward" and included a presentation by the committee of its findings and recommendations. In August 2012, the Libraries Going Forward committee met again to consider a suggestion that the STARS team be restarted as a complement to the Libraries Going Forward group. The Libraries Going Forward committee concurred with this recommendation and will reorganize at least a portion of itself as the STARS committee.

WHAT REMAINS TO BE DONE

STARS took the RCLS to an important point. With great vigor and creativity, the STARS team articulated a vision of customer-focused library services delivered by well-trained and highly motivated library staff. The recommendations and actions that came forward from this group had an immediate positive impact on the culture of the RCLS as well as throughout LSSI. Most of those practices have been in place ever since (even if all staff do not know where they came from).

The challenge ahead is for library management and staff to find ways to routinize the quality improvement loop and begin to saturate the values of the organization through every employee. It will be important to find new ways to solicit customer feedback and to find ways to apply those comments and responses to improve the quality of library service. Library managers and the management team are committed to finding ways to orient, train, evaluate, and coach staff to constantly reflect the highest shared values of the organization and to find ways to eliminate needless tasks and streamline procedures. Through these and other methods, STARS will continue to be an important element in our ongoing drive to make customer-focused service our highest priority.

REFERENCES

Lundin, S. C., & Christensen, J. (2000). *Fish! A remarkable way to boost morale and improve results.* New York: Hyperion.

National Institute of Standards and Technology. (2012). *Malcolm Baldridge Performance Excellence Program.* Retrieved from http://www.nist.gov/baldrige/

National Retail Federation. (2012). *Certification in customer service.* Retrieved from http://www.nrffoundation.com/content/certification-customer-service

Spector, R., & McCarthy, P. (2005). *The Nordstrom way to customer service excellence: A handbook for implementing great customer service in your organization.* Hoboken, NJ: Wiley.

5

The Collaborative Conversation: Connecting Libraries and Readers Using Web 2.0 Tools

JUDI REPMAN
Georgia Southern University

On August 13, 2012, Otis Chandler blogged that Goodreads—a social networking site for readers, book lovers, and authors—had reached the milestone of 10 million members, who had "shelved" 360 million books. In the same post, Chandler reported that Goodreads' five largest shared interest groups—Paranormal Romance and Urban Fantasy, The Sword and Laser, Boxall's 1001 Books You Must Read before You Die, The Next Best Book Club, and Poetry—boasted from 7,771 to 12,507 members each. On the same date the comparable website LibraryThing[1] boasted 1,557,479 members, while the most active reviewer on Shelfari had posted 6,331 reviews. Impressive numbers and impressive activity on the part of book lovers of all ages! This chapter provides an overview of how a wide range of interactive Web 2.0 tools can involve patrons of all libraries in conversations about books and reading. Specifically, this chapter focuses on the practical application of tools such as Goodreads, which have clearly struck a chord with library patrons who want to interact with others about books and reading. Examples of libraries using generic social networking tools such as Twitter and Facebook are shared, including a discussion of the resources needed to establish connections and maintain links with library patrons using Web 2.0 tools. Use of social networking tools developed specifically for book lovers (Goodreads, LibraryThing, and Shelfari) and their use in library settings are described, followed by a discussion of the use of the tools for readers' advisory and reverse readers' advisory. The chapter closes with a brief discussion of the implications for library practices that might result from the use of these tools, such as patron-driven acquisitions.

As Wright and Bass (2010) note, "These environments cry out for knowledgeable, reader-focused library workers to participate in them, implementing tags and creating lists that meet readers' needs, sharing our own input as readers, reviewers, book-talkers and lively conversationalists" (p. 10). After all, what library wouldn't want an online reading group with even 700 members, much less 7,000? Today we have tools on hand that will allow us to extend our reach to readers 24/7/365 and interact with our reading patrons in ways that were not possible just a few short years ago. This kind of outreach redefines the concept of customer service, particularly in the area of readers' advisory services (Naik, 2012; Repman & Jones, 2012; Tarulli, 2011).

WEB 2.0 TOOLS AND LIBRARY PRACTICE

Web 2.0, usually defined as the read/write web (O'Reilly, 2005), has much to offer libraries at all levels. "Traditional" library websites are passive, read-only experiences for library users, where users might be able to look up information or locate needed resources, but these offer few, if any, opportunities for participation, interaction, or conversation. Many librarians (and many more of our current and potential patrons) use sites such as Facebook and Twitter for communicating, interacting, and learning throughout the course of a day. Today's Web 2.0 tools share one common characteristic—they focus on the user and the ability of the user to participate in some form of interaction as much or as little as he or she chooses. As libraries have created Facebook pages and Twitter feeds to push out information to patrons, they have discovered that library users today want and expect a more interactive, immediate, and participatory experience (Petit, 2011; Repman & Jones, 2012; Tarulli, 2011). A recent survey by the Pew Internet and American Life project reports that information consumption increased from 7.4 to 11.8 hours per day between 1960 and 2008. The same study found that between May 2011 and February 2012, smartphone ownership increased from 35% to 48% among the 89% of adult Americans who now own a cell phone (Rainie, 2012). Rainie (2012) highlights this as a challenge for educators, which translates easily into a related challenge for librarians: Rather than individuals coming to the library, the library must go to the individual. And going to the individual today involves the use of a wide range of tools and strategies. Using no-cost and ubiquitous tools, today's libraries can meet the needs of current patrons as well as patrons who may never walk through the door of the local library. Naik (2012) characterizes the discussions on many of these user-focused social networking sites as "gloriously messy" (p. 323). Participation may require attitude and perception checks on the part of library staff, since most forms of informal and formal control simply do not exist on the read/write web. Other challenges exist in finding a balance in resource allocation between our brick-and-mortar libraries and the new interactive library, without boundaries, that exists in cyberspace. In this context, resource allocation must include staff time as a resource.

The amount of staff time required to maintain a vibrant presence on social networking sites should not be discounted (Petit, 2011), but these tools have the same advantages for library staff that they have for our reading public. The tools are free or very low cost; they can be accessed from any place with an Internet connection; and they are simple to use. A library using Web 2.0 tools can also take advantage of expertise beyond front-line library staff. Perhaps a tech services staff member has a particular interest in mysteries. That individual could facilitate the online discussion of the mysteries through the library's Facebook or Goodreads social networking space. Fortunately (or unfortunately), many of us are used to reading work-related e-mail at home in the evenings or on weekends. A library with an active participatory online community will find that staff members will be engaging with readers using those tools outside of standard work hours. But given that many librarians were attracted to the field because of a deep desire to link books with readers, it is possible that job satisfaction might actually increase as more patrons and more new patrons come to rely on the expertise of librarians and use library services and programs.

GENERIC OPTIONS: BLOGS, FACEBOOK, AND TWITTER

Blogging has become a widely used Web 2.0 tool. Early blogs were primarily one-way communication, where the blogger expounded on a topic of his or her own choosing, with readers being able to append comments to the post. Blogs still work that way, but updated blog software offers many more capabilities. With new magazine-like RSS/blog readers and aggregators such as Zite, Flipboard, and Scoop.it becoming more common, library blogs may find their traffic increase, particularly traffic from readers who do not live in a library's service area but who are looking for curated, informed discussions of books on a wide range of topics. The Denver Public Library[2] hosts a range of topic-focused book blogs, which are aggregated on a Books Blog page. Through the use of tags and appeal terms, these blog posts appear in search engine results, extending the reach of the blogging library staff member and drawing potentially more individuals into the conversation (Naik, 2012). The Bulldog Readers Blog[3] demonstrates how an elementary library blogger can connect students, reading, and Web 2.0 tools through one site. The school librarian known as Xena's Mom uses her blog, Librarian's Quest,[4] as a virtual place where students, educators, and parents can use the comment aspect to share current reading and other thoughts about books. Blogs can make use of guest bloggers so that no individual is responsible for daily or weekly blog posts. Rotating the responsibility for blog posts among library staff members, possibly including volunteers or library board members, ensures wider participation and gives patrons the chance to make wide-ranging connections. While much of the use of social networking seems to be based on "friends" with like interests, exposing readers of a library blog to a wide range of opinions and recommendations should be seen as a positive approach.

Facebook is now so widely known and used that features such as "like" and "friend" have become part of our everyday vocabulary and similar features are incorporated in many other web tools. Facebook pages (as opposed to personal Facebook sites) offer many opportunities for libraries to interact with communities (Fredrick, 2012; King, 2011). The New York Public Library Facebook page[5] has over 65,000 likes. The page features regularly changing interactive features and news updates. Many libraries, including the Seattle Public Library,[6] use their Facebook page to share reading lists and ask for responses to questions such as "What's the best book to read on a beautiful summer day?" Use of Facebook by school libraries does raise issues, such as use by children under the age of 13 (prohibited by Facebook's own policies) and the filtering and blocking software used in school library environments. Fredrick (2012) points out that while school librarians must be aware of these restrictions, a Facebook page can still serve as an excellent way to reach the parents of students under the age of 13. She also notes that much of our use of social networking occurs on home computers, so a Facebook page can still provide significant outreach and customer service, even though a school librarian may not be able to access the page using school computers. Parents frequently want recommendations for books for their children, and a school library Facebook page could include parent book clubs, with teachers and librarians participating and sharing their expertise. The Creekview High School Media Center page, maintained by Buffy Hamilton, is a good example of the thoughtful use of Facebook in a high school setting.[7]

Twitter, the microblogging social network that limits posts to 140 characters, continues its rapid growth and adoption by educators and librarians for a variety of purposes. Twitter networks are based on two tools. First, you can "follow" other twitter users so when that user tweets or retweets, the post appears in your twitter feed. The @ symbol is used to send direct messages to other twitter users, so a patron could send a direct message to whatever librarian has been assigned to respond to direct messages sent via Twitter. The second major tool for libraries interested in using Twitter to connect with library patrons is based on the hashtag (#). It is simple to search Twitter feeds for posts with specific hashtags. A hashtag can be used to indicate a hot topic, a book group, a book title or author, or a library's name. Unlike subject headings, hashtags are constantly being developed. Occasional users of Twitter are not always familiar with hashtags as a way to organize and access tweets.

Twitter book groups are becoming very popular. Once the time parameters are set (as in, "We will discuss this book from Monday, August 20 through Sunday, August 26"), the book club organizer can then specify a hashtag that is added to all book discussion-related tweets. Penguin's Twitter Book Club describes how to set this up.[8] Jeff Howe (2012) created the 1book140 Twitter book club based on librarian Nancy Pearl's idea that everyone in Seattle should read and discuss the same book. Howe's Twitter book club has attracted participants from around the world, who participate as much as they want, when they want. When Howe described this experience in May 2012, 1book140 had over 64,000 members. 1book140 is a partnership with a commercial entity, which might be a model for a library to consider adopting.

THE MAJOR BOOK-RELATED SOCIAL NETWORKING SITES

Goodreads,[9] LibraryThing,[10] and Shelfari[11] are far and away the most popular book-focused social networking sites. Each offers spaces for individuals to "catalog" or "shelve" his or her own book collection, mechanisms to rate and review those books, and ever-changing and ever-growing communities for interaction among other participants in the network. Both Goodreads and LibraryThing offer tools to integrate their services with library catalogs, or libraries can establish their own spaces within the sites. The Scottsdale Public Library has a page on its library site with Goodreads staff reviews as well as other Goodreads reviews. The bottom of the page encourages library patrons to write a review, suggest an item for purchase, or order a title through interlibrary loan.[12] LibraryThing hosts multiple groups for librarians, with the largest being Librarians Who LibraryThing. This virtual discussion group touches on many topics, including readers' advisory and how to use LibraryThing's features to engage library patrons. LibraryThing for Libraries[13] is a suite of tools that integrates LibraryThing with a library's online catalog. These features are used by the Brisbane (Australia) Grammar School Library catalog to allow its patrons to search and sort by LibraryThing tags, read and write reviews, and browse the virtual shelves of the Grammar School Library. The Valdosta (Georgia) State University Library takes advantages of Shelfari's ability to display virtual bookshelves to highlight topical collections such as a group of children's books about wildlife and young adult novels.[14] Widgets that have been developed for these social networking sites make it straightforward for nonprogrammers to embed virtual book shelves, a constantly changing list of reviews, and so on, within library websites.

Each site described provides members with the ability to set up private book discussion groups. Private groups may be used to facilitate book discussions in a more controlled setting. Sturgis East Freshmen make use of a members-only Goodreads group to discuss required summer reading.[15] The page for this discussion group includes embedded author videos. While membership in the Sturgis East group is restricted, members can invite participants, so it is easy to see how teachers and students from other schools might become involved in a broader discussion. Given the prominent role that many authors play on social networking sites for book lovers, it is possible that an author might even participate in the online discussions. Howe (2012) noted that authors such as Neil Gaiman and Margaret Atwood have been participants in the 1book140 Twitter discussions.

Use of any social networking site does require preplanning and a review of library policies. In addition to the standard concerns over privacy and use of language that some patrons might find offensive, advertising and links to commercial entities should be areas of consideration when libraries incorporate these sites into their programming. LibraryThing and Shelfari are owned wholly or partly by Amazon.com, so use of some features on each site includes a direct link to the Amazon site. Most school library acceptable-use policies prohibit access to "shopping." Many library policies prohibit advertising, although these policies may have been written when advertising meant putting a commercial vendor's name on the library bulletin board. Some schools or organizations place restrictions on social networking and being able to "friend" students or patrons. The ability to use sites such as Goodreads, LibraryThing, and Shelfari for academic purposes provides an opportunity for discussion and review of such policies. Being able to present positive examples of these tools in action is an important part of the policy review and redevelopment process.

READERS' ADVISORY AND REVERSE READERS' ADVISORY

Readers' advisory, where professional librarians offer reading suggestions to patrons, has a long tradition in library settings. Readers' advisory can take the form of an individual recommendation when a patron approaches a librarian for a suggestion for a book "just like the one I just finished" or for a book "that's a great adventure story set in Alaska." Given the number of patrons who visit libraries and the limited available staff, readers' advisory is often somewhat generic, offered in the form of lists of recommended reading or websites that make recommendations based on similarities or the next book in a series. The Kent (Michigan) Library District provides a web-based "What's Next: Books in Series" database,[16] while the Hennepin County Library offers an "If You Like This Author" database.[17] Sutton (2012) reviewed six public library websites in Indiana to try to identify use of Web 2.0 tools for readers' advisory. She found some use of a wide range of tools, including a dedicated readers' advisory webpage, Facebook, Twitter, Blogs, YouTube, online book clubs, online book reviews, and integration of LibraryThing or Goodreads into the library's web offerings. Sutton found considerable interest in the use of these tools, but only one library (Greenwood Public Library) had instituted a committee to try to systematize the use of Web 2.0 tools for readers' advisory purposes. While beyond the scope of this chapter, many new iterations of library catalog software have incorporated readers' advisory features (Tarulli, 2011). As Tarulli notes, incorporating social networking readers' advisory features into library catalogs help patrons to see libraries as social spaces. She believes that readers' advisory can and should leave the physical boundaries of our libraries and become a conversation that involves a broad spectrum of current users, new users, and library staff members.

Wright and Bass (2010) present many suggestions for using ubiquitous Web 2.0 tools for readers' advisory, pointing out that "the very latest tech trends are finally catching up to the traditional values and goals of high-touch readers' advisory" (p. 9). Their suggestions include preparing personalized reading lists, which would require the use of an online form completed by patrons to indicate reading interests and preferences, through the use of Twitter and Facebook. The Williamsburg Public Library has provided personalized reading lists using an online reader profile form.[18] Most consumers have at least a passing acquaintance with this model based on Amazon's use of "Customers who viewed this item also viewed" feature. The Cuyahoge County Public Library hosted a very successful readers' advisory day on the library's Facebook page. The event attracted over 200 participants, and the library's page acquired 300 new "likes" (Rua, 2011). With the sophistication of the book-focused social networking sites described here, readers can continually engage in do-it-yourself readers' advisory by searching using tags and other descriptors (Naik, 2012). Of course, the social networking sites provide readers with access to millions of other readers who will eagerly offer suggestions for that next book to read.

No doubt that everyone reading this chapter has engaged in reverse readers' advisory, where the person who is on the receiving end of our recommendation turns the tables and recommends a title (or author or an entire list of titles) back to us. Using interactive Web 2.0 tools and social networking sites, libraries can create two-way conversations just like this around books and reading. The library can be an important destination for readers that goes far beyond looking in the online catalog to request a title. Using Web 2.0 tools from blogs to Twitter can facilitate the development of a vibrant community that links library users of any age with library staff to discuss and share books and build chains of readers. Few of us have access to the resources to create an experience like Oprah's Book Club 2.0,[19] but we can use it as a model for our own services. We can embed author interviews from sites such as YouTube, publishers' sites, or authors' home pages, and we can use a range of free and easy-to-use podcasting tools to create experiences that "speak" to our local patrons. The Seattle BiblioCafe[20] is one well-developed example of this kind of initiative (Wright & Bass, 2010). Libraries should not overlook the opportunity to piggyback local efforts on large virtual initiatives such as Oprah's Book Club 2.0 or 1book140. A library could host a face-to-face discussion related to the online efforts or perhaps even provide local programming to enhance and extend the activities of any of the online groups.

Naik (2012) completed a master's thesis research project applying readers' advisory concepts to how Goodreads is used. Given her limited sample size, she concluded that Goodreads discussions exhibited most of the characteristics of traditional readers' advisory. She identified the use of appeal terms within reviews on the site and highlighted positive reviews, suggestions for read-alikes or books with similar themes, and social reciprocity (reverse readers' advisory, where a participant responds to a reviewer, then makes a suggestion back to the reviewer) as features of the Goodreads version of readers' advisory. Naik notes that there is a high level of trust among participants on Goodreads (the "friending" concept) and concludes that librarians have much to contribute to these readers' advisory interactions. Naik suggests that the readers' advisory model that has developed on Goodreads is "as if there were a book discussion happening right at the shelf, right in front of [the patron's] favorite book, in which not only are people discussing the word at hand but giving profuse suggestions to read other writers and works" (p. 322). Naik indicates that exploring online readers' advisory as it has developed in the world of Web 2.0 is a fruitful area for further research. This research could help librarians reconceptualize readers' advisory to meet the needs of the networked individuals described in surveys conducted by the Pew Internet and American Life Project (Rainie, 2012).

FROM CONVERSATION TO
COMMITMENT: PATRON-DRIVEN ACQUISITIONS

Librarians also have an opportunity to use social networking technologies to refine our approach to collection development. Although funding has decreased in these days of vanishing library materials budgets, professional collection development continues to be based on review sources, professional judgment, and knowledge of the community. Given the numbers of persons participating on sites such as Goodreads, it appears that librarians can now get a much better sense of community needs and interests. Anderson (2011) offers a commonsense definition of patron-driving acquisition: "In a largely digital environment, it's increasing possible to let library users find and identify desired documents prior to the library's purchase of them, and for the library to pay only for what its patrons find and actually use" (para. 2). Patron-drive acquisitions have been a topic of discussion and research in academic libraries (see, e.g., Hodges, Preston, & Hamilton, 2010; Nixon, Freeman, & Ward, 2010). Academic libraries have had very positive results with this approach, particularly in terms of meeting the just-in-time, "I needed it yesterday" needs of undergraduate students and developing e-book collections (Hodges et al., 2010). Public and school libraries can use this research to support their efforts to acquire materials based on patron requests. While this might not require the same paradigm shift for librarians in public and school libraries, social networking sites and Web 2.0 tools provide extensive options for librarians to systematically engage in patron-driven acquisition.

CONCLUDING THOUGHTS

Many of us were afraid that reading would decrease as brick-and-mortar book stores closed and libraries decreased hours and services. We might also have been afraid that library use would decrease in the age of Google, Facebook, and Amazon.com. None of those predictions have come to pass. Reading in many different formats is clearly alive and well, and the conversation about books, authors, and reading now takes place through the standard Tuesday morning book group as well as through mega sites such as LibraryThing and Oprah's Book Club 2.0. It's exciting to think about all of the different places where we can engage in readers' advisory conversations with patrons who are not bound by time or place. Not only are the Web 2.0 tools described in this chapter easy to use, but they are also interconnected. Once you post on your blog, you can tweet the blog post, create a link to it on your Facebook page, and then sit back and wait for comments, responses, ideas, suggestions, and new ideas to come to you and to everybody else involved in the conversation. Customer service, meet Readers' Advisory 2.0!

NOTES

1. http://www.librarything.com/zeitgeist.
2. http://denverlibrary.org/category/blogs/books-blog.

3. http://bellbulldogreaders.edublogs.org.
4. http://librariansquest.blogspot.com.
5. http://www.facebook.com/newyorkpubliclibrary.
6. http://www.facebook.com/SeattlePublicLibrary.
7. http://www.facebook.com/pages/The-Unquiet-Library-Creekview-High-School-Media-Center/31676317923.
8. http://us.penguingroup.com/static/pages/features/twitter_book_club/index.html.
9. http://www.Goodreads.com.
10. http://www.librarything.com.
11. http://www.shelfari.com.
12. http://www.scottsdalelibrary.org/Goodreads_reviews.
13. http://www.librarything.com/forlibraries/.
14. http://www.valdosta.edu/library/about/shelfari.shtml.
15. http://www.Goodreads.com/group/show/69464-sturgis-east-freshmen-summer-reading.
16. http://ww2.kdl.org/libcat/whatsnext.asp.
17. http://www.hclib.org/pub/bookspace/findagoodbook.cfm.
18. http://www.wrl.org/books-and-reading/adults/find-good-book/looking-good-book-reader-profile-forms.
19. http://www.oprah.com/packages/oprahs-book-club-2.html.
20. http://www.spl.org/Audio/podcasts/podcast.spl_author_feed.xml.

REFERENCES

Anderson, R. (2011, May 31). *What patron-driven acquisition (PDA) does and doesn't mean: An FAQ.* Retrieved from http://scholarlykitchen.sspnet.org/2011/05/31/what-patron-driven-acquisition-pda-does-and-doesnt-mean-an-faq/
Chandler, O. (2102, August 13). *Ten million thank yous!* Retrieved from http://www.Goodreads.com/blog/show/380-ten-million-thank-yous.
Fredrick, K. (2012). Sharing your library with Facebook pages. *School Library Monthly, 28*(5), 24–26.
Hodges, D., Preston, C., & Hamilton, M. J. (2010). Patron-initiated collection development: Progress of a paradigm shift. *Collection Management, 35*(3–4), 208–221.
Howe, J. (2012, May 18). Books with 140 characters. *New York Times.* Retrieved from http://www.nytimes.com/2012/05/20/books/review/books-with-140-characters.html?pagewanted=all
King, D. L. (2011). *Facebook for libraries.* Retrieved from http://americanlibrariesmagazine.org/features/05272011/facebook-libraries
Naik, Y. (2012). Finding good reads on Goodreads: Readers take RA into their own hands. *Reference & User Services Quarterly, 51*, 319–323.
Nixon, J. M., Freeman, R. S., & Ward, S. M. (2010). Patron-drive acquisitions: An introduction and literature review. *Collection Management, 35*(3–4), 119–124.

O'Reilly, T. (2005). What is Web 2.0: Design patterns and business models for the next generation of software. Available online at http://oreilly.com/web2/archive/what-is-web-20.html.

Petit, J. (2011). Twitter and Facebook for user collection requests. *Collection Management, 36*(4), 253–258.

Rainie, L. (2012, August). *Networked learners.* Retrieved from http://pewinternet.org/Presentations/2012/Aug/Networked-Learners.aspx

Repman, J., & Jones, S. (2012). Reader's advisory for net-gen students. *Library Media Connection, 30*(4), 34–35.

Rua, R. J. (2011). Mission connect. *Library Journal, 136*(8), 26.

Sutton, C. (2012, March). *Library 2.0 and readers advisory.* Retrieved from http://theriffedlibrarian.blogspot.com/2012/03/library-20–and-readers-advisory.html

Tarulli, L. (2011). Readers' service and the library catalog: Coming of age fiction? Or non-fiction? *Reference and User Services Quarterly, 51*, 115–118.

Wright, D., & Bass, A. (2010). No reader is an island: New strategies for readers' advisory. *Alki, 26*(3), 9–10.

6

Improving Customer Service by Utilizing an Existing Technology Innovatively

Adriana Gonzalez
The Texas A&M University Libraries

The library landscape is changing at a rapid pace, with libraries as a place remaining an important component. With the changing library landscape, a greater demand is placed on study space conducive to individual learning and studying, as well as group study. For large academic libraries, space management and the balance between study space and materials is critical, especially as group learning and collaboration are incorporated into teaching curricula. Howe and Strauss (2000) point out that there is a "new focus on teamwork; students prefer working together rather than alone." The new emphasis of group learning and collaboration has direct implications for libraries, since they are now seen as more than just a place for books. Despite this trend, university infrastructures are unable to continue building or expand existing building space due to funding, time, and space constraints. It goes without saying that this is an ongoing challenge. So how does a large academic library manage such a high-demand resource such as study space in a fair and effective manner?

The Texas A&M University (TAMU) Libraries demonstrate how this can be accomplished through an effective space management model using an existing technology typically utilized in another customer service industry: the industry, restaurants; the technology, pagers. What this ultimately accomplished was improved customer service and satisfaction, which is the libraries' main objective: to provide excellent customer service.

THE PROBLEM

In the middle of the 2000–2010 period, the TAMU was experiencing significant growth in enrollment, without the growth in infrastructure to match.

57

In 2007, on a campus of approximately 40,000 students, 2,000 faculty, and 2,500 staff, the library was feeling the pressure for needed space. Students wanted and needed group study space, which was provided in dedicated group study rooms with varying capacities of 4 to 12 persons, as well as open group study space. There were 44 group study rooms and open study space for approximately 449 individuals, yet not all the open study space was conducive to group study. The 44 group study rooms were located in the Library Annex, which was open from Sunday at noon to Friday at 9:00 PM (24/5), from Saturday at 9:00 AM to 9:00 PM, and continuously during finals week (24/7). The Library Annex is adjoined to the main campus library, the Sterling C. Evans Library, via skybridge. The Evans library, however, was not open extended hours, making the Library Annex the main library for students to study during the night hours.

The problem was the lack of a system to effectively manage the limited group study rooms with the high demand of students needing that space. There was much stress experienced by students waiting and by the staff at the service desk. To begin addressing this need, various models were tried before reaching the pager system as a solution. It is important to mention these previous models because so much in a solution is based on what has been learned and tried. Additionally, one of the previous models may still have relevance and utility at other libraries, if not tried already.

PREVIOUS MODELS

One model for managing the group study rooms, then as most recent, required that a room key be checked out from the service desk. The use of a room key was the longest-used model before the pagers. The group study rooms were then checked out on a first-come, first-served basis. The loan period was for no more than 4 hours per day per person. While the use of a room key was the most effective before pagers, there were definite drawbacks. Students quickly figured out how to circumvent the loan policies. If in groups, a second or third student would then check out the key as soon as it was returned by the first student. While this was not breaking any policies, in practice this created a monopoly on rooms, with certain groups potentially occupying a room for most of the day, especially in larger groups. Another drawback to this model is that, without effective policy enforcement, there was an ineffective manner in which to monitor whether true groups were utilizing the room or just an individual. While we discouraged individuals from occupying a group study room, without an effective monitoring system, it was not possible to then enforce the policy. Finally, another significant drawback was students checking out a group study room to simply store their belongings while they conducted other business on campus.

While we understood why students would do this on a campus as large as the TAMU, this was not at all the intended use of the rooms. Lockers were available for checkout; however, they were all located in the Evans library, which further complicated the problem since that building was not open through the night. Yet, even without those drawbacks, the room key model created other problems—the biggest: long, winding lines trailing around the desk and down a long hallway or large crowds standing around a small lobby area waiting for a room. Now, the overall problem was not solely a space management problem; it became a wait-list management problem, creating much customer service dissatisfaction. This became not only a problem for the students waiting for a group study room but a problem for those studying in open study space. Students could end up waiting for hours, sometimes for more hours than they would be permitted to occupy a room, which further added to the overall problem because it thus became a time management problem from the perspective of the student. The problems do not end there. This was also a great problem for the desk staff, who were mostly student workers and found it incredibly stressful managing limited space and many unhappy individuals. It is difficult to believe that given all these drawbacks, before the pagers, this was the most effective way of managing the group study rooms and withheld the longest amount of time.

A second model tried utilizing sign-up sheets and still checking out a room key. This model was ineffective because it did not offer any crowd management. While it decreased waiting lines, it still required individuals to stay nearby and wait for their names to be called. The lobby space of the Library Annex is small and contained between the entrance/gates and the desk, thereby limiting the space to about 5 by 20 feet. Again, this was not entirely convenient or effective because the wait time was not necessarily decreased and waiting patrons were still disruptive to individuals studying in the nearby open study space. Furthermore, the desk staff had to loudly announce a student's name, several times. This caused greater disruption to those studying in open study space, but it also created concern over privacy, since student names were being loudly called out. This certainly did not eliminate stress for the desk staff.

A third model involved scheduling the rooms and requiring a room key for checkout. While this seemed the fairest way of distributing the space, it was not effective if there were no-shows or if an individual left a room early. There was not a systematic or effective way of tracking changes to the schedule. Another drawback was that this was done with paper and pencil, making it impossible for a student to check availability ahead of time. This did not help with time management.

A fourth model adopted an open-door system by not requiring that a room key be checked out. This was probably the most ineffective model, since there was a sharp increase in student-to-student conflict. Students would see a room empty but with someone else's belongings and decide to occupy the room and remove the other person's belongings. This type of behavior happened frequently, frequently resulting in staff intervention and mediation. This model was very quickly abandoned.

Through most of these models, one of the biggest challenges came from trying to manage the long wait times. It was not at all uncommon on such a large campus to have a couple of hundred students waiting in any of these models. To further confirm the demand for group study rooms and the unhappiness being experienced by students, data taken from the LibQUAL+ service satisfaction survey were reviewed, which added support to taking further action to improve customer service overall.

REVIEW OF EXISTING DATA

While anecdotal evidence is important—and, in my opinion, oftentimes very accurate—it is equally important to look at actual numbers and actual feedback to have a more complete picture. It is advisable that some sort of data be collected and analyzed, even if not from a program such as LibQUAL+. Since LibQUAL+ data were readily available at the TAMU and had been collected for several years, the survey was a natural place to start in looking for data specifically about the group study rooms. For those not familiar with LibQUAL+, it is a service satisfaction measurement tool for libraries, with four factors, one of which is "Library as Place."

As far back as 2003, LibQUAL+ survey results document the demand for more group study space. The comments very clearly and directly voice the students' dissatisfaction with the lack of space management and the lack of wait times. A small sample of comments received by students from 2003 to 2011 regarding group study rooms follow (written exactly as they were by students):

"Line for study rooms is outrageous sometimes at 6–9 at night."
"It seems to me that almost every single time I go with a study group to get a study group room (during finals), there are none available."
"The study room allocation currently is not very efficient."
"I wish there were more rooms available to check out so that they can be used."

"Finding a way to not wait so long for a group study room would be nice."
"Need more study room; they are always so full."

With glaring evidence of a problem needing immediate attention, the TAMU Libraries began research on an innovative approach to resolve the problem. When we hear the word *innovation*, oftentimes the imagery behind that is some new start-of-the-art gadget with bells and whistles, operating at light speed. Yet, in the more pure sense of the word, innovation is thinking creatively, thinking outside the box, and taking advantage of existing resources. And that was exactly what was done.

IMPLEMENTATION OF PAGER SYSTEM

Without reinventing the wheel for customer service, the library began looking at other customer service industries that faced similar challenges: limited space, large numbers of people. Hospitals and restaurants seemed the mostly likely candidates, with the latter mirroring libraries the closest since there was a quicker turn-around rate of space and a little more predictable use of space, unlike that with hospitals. It was noted that handheld wireless one-way pagers were utilized among non-fast-food restaurants. This was beneficial not only to the restaurants in managing wait lists but to the customers since they felt served and informed of their space need. This also meant that customers did not need to stay close to the hostess for direction. And it was fair since pagers were distributed on a first-come, first-served basis. Additionally, customers with special requests at restaurants were still served but with the understanding that their wait time might be extended. This also fit nicely within the library's need since some group study rooms came equipped with a computer, large table, or whiteboard. A student could still place a request for one of these special group study rooms with the understanding that his or her wait time may be extended. The student would still receive a pager and be called once the requested group study room became available. Interestingly enough, the mere fact of being handed a pager was found to increase customer service satisfaction. Students felt like they were being helped, even if their actual wait time did not decrease.

The research began. One of the primary factors was to find an effective pager system with a broad receptor range that was not impeded by steel-building construction with multibuilding range. No easy feat given that the Library Annex is a six-story building surrounded by other equally sized campus buildings. This was an important factor because students could be in the library but also be in the Evans library or even on the sixth floor of the Library Annex or even a neighboring building, such as the student commons building. Whatever the case, the signal had to reach them. Another important factor was the space necessary to keep the system storage and recharging tower. The equipment would need to occupy a minimal amount of space at the main service counter, which was limited. The counter space housed two desk staff with individual work stations, circulation equipment, and various other necessary desk pieces and paperwork. The paging system would need to be easily accessible by both desk staff at all times, requiring minimal movement with close electrical outlets. Finally, the pager system would need to have a way of sending an alarm to the student if out of range. This was a tall order, and the expectation was great. Would such a pager system exist? Was there a vendor who could possibly make this happen for the TAMU?

The research continued. There were two main pager styles: a coaster style or a tapered style. In restaurants, the coaster style seems to be more popular. Yet, given the desk needs, the tapered style seemed the most feasible since it occupied the least amount of space. After reviewing several vendors, JTECH (http://www.jtech.com) was chosen, and a tapered-style pager was bought. The total system price, at that time, for 30 pagers was $3,330. The transmitter was $600; the charging towers, each fitting 20 pagers, were $240 each; and each GuestPass pager was $75. The system was easily installed. The pagers transmitted to approximately half a mile and included a distinctive "out of range" beep to inform the student if he or she went out of range. The pager system was implemented in fall 2007. The decision to implement it at the Library Annex was made because it held the greatest number of group study rooms, was open the longest hours, and was a centrally located library on campus. Most important, it posed a fair and efficient mechanism in managing the limited space against the high demand for that space. Success!

The easiest part of the implementation was, unbelievably, the training to use the system. The pager system was easy to install, and training took about 5 minutes to teach someone how to set and reset a pager. Process training took longer, of course, but even that took about 10 minutes. Each pager had to be calibrated by the vendor to match its corresponding charging tower, since we had two towers. Therefore, each pager was labeled with a number and its own barcode so that it could be checked out to the student. As the saying goes, "the devil is in the details," and the process of issuing a pager was critical to its success, but it also created a minor challenge, which is talked about later in the chapter.

COLLECTION OF MORE DATA

As librarians, we love data, we love to collect data, we love to review data, and we love to use data—on almost anything. As soon as the pagers were implemented, usage data were collected. A snapshot of one of the busiest times for room use—the week before finals and the week of finals—was taken and is depicted three different ways in Figures 6.1 and 6.2 and Table 6.1. The data supported similar findings by Gardner and Eng (2005), as well as by Sheesley (2002), that students prefer studying in the evening and late-night hours. To no surprise and in support of anecdotal evidence, the data also reflected that the use of pagers was greatest during finals week and that wait times were longest during the evening and late-night hours. A notable trend depicted by the data was that the busiest time for group study rooms is the 2 weeks leading up to final exam days. Table 6.1 represents the combined data from Figures 6.1 and 6.2. Ironically, the implementation of the pagers did not decrease wait times. It did however help with the management of space, student time, wait lists, and desk staff stress.

LibQUAL+ data were again reviewed. Oddly, from the survey comments, pagers are not mentioned either positively or negatively at all since their implementation in 2007. One observation of the survey comments, however, is that the group study room needs seemingly became more specific, as reflected in a small sample from 2010 through 2011 (written exactly as they were by students):

> "Study rooms are the resource that I use the most and if they could be more comfortable then I would be much more satisfied with the library. And by comfortable I mean the chairs are usually old and worn out and

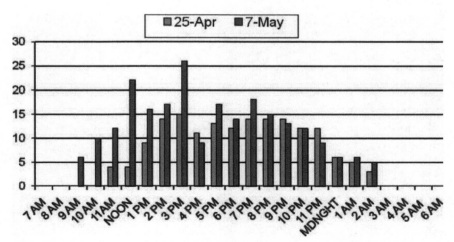

Figure 6.1. The number of pagers issued by time of day. Source: Data first presented by Mosley, Carter, Desai, and Arant-Kaspar (2007), published in Gonzalez (2012).

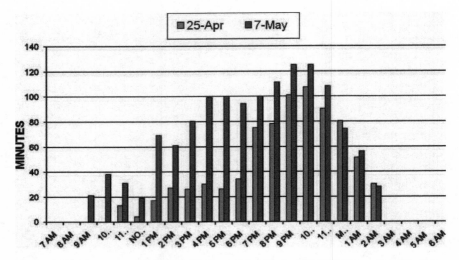

Figure 6.2.   The average wait time by time of day. Source: Data first presented by Mosley, Carter, Desai, and Arant-Kaspar (2007), published by Gonzalez (2012).

Table 6.1.   Number of Pagers Issued and Average Wait Times by Day: April 23–May 8, 2007

Date	No. of Pagers Issued	Average Wait Time, Minutes
Mon, Apr 23	189	59
Tue, Apr 24	167	56
Wed, Apr 25	195	55
Thu, Apr 26	90	17
Fri, Apr 27	0	0
Sat, Apr 28	0	0
Sun, Apr 29	29	10
Mon, Apr 30	47	16
Tue, May 1	72	26
Wed, May 2	193	39
Thu, May 3	252	87
Fri, May 4a	38	29
Sat, May 5	184	50
Sun, May 6	256	98
Mon, May 7[a]	263	76
Tue, May 8[a]	278	49

Source: Data first presented by Mosley, Carter, Desai, and Arant-Kaspar (2007), published by Gonzalez (2012).

[a]Final exam dates.

if there were computers in more of them it would be very convenient as
well."

"Some of the study rooms in the ground floor do not have signals for mobile phones. It would be nice if this is addressed."

"The group study rooms in the Evans are extremely hot. No air flow between 8 people makes it pretty hard to focus."

Mind you, these rooms have not changed in all these years, so it is interesting that while one major problem was addressed, students now noticed the
other problems that have always existed. Why are pagers never mentioned
in the LibQUAL+ results, even if searching under terms such as "restaurant
thingy," "coaster," or "buzzer"? The absence begs the question of what the
real impact was on customer service. In most recent data, a growing frustration about wait times is now more clearly evidenced.

STUDENT REACTIONS AND FURTHERING THE MISSION

Despite the fact that pagers are not at all mentioned in the LibQUAL+ data,
anecdotally, the reaction from students was positive and optimistic and had
the "cool" factor. By far, the pager model has been the most effective model
used for managing the group study rooms and wait lists at the Library Annex
and has withstood the test of time. Ultimately, the success of implementing a
pager system for such a high-demand resource helped the ultimate objective
of the university libraries by improving a critical customer service and thus
furthering the mission in providing students with a more positive learning
environment and experience.

The benefits of the pager system were immediately experienced by students and desk staff. First, students no longer had to remain close to the
service desk. In turn, this eliminated the need for desk staff to call out anyone's name, the need for students to wait in the small lobby area, and the
creation of long, trailing lines of students. Students were now free to move
about within the library buildings and neighboring buildings. In turn, the
students were given the ability to manage their time better and feel more in
control over their time. Additionally, there were perceived improvements
to service. Students felt better served as they walked away with something
in their hands. They trusted the pager and trusted that their number would
be called. The pagers were a familiar technology, used in their favorite
eateries, and the system had not failed them before; therefore, trusting the
system at the library came naturally, without question, and without necessary training.

LESSONS LEARNED

You might be asking yourself where the pitfalls are with this system—a very valid question, because no model is perfect. The implementation of the pager system did create new challenges. While actual wait time did not decrease, this seemingly did not resurface as an issue, at least not immediately. Keep in mind that the campus is very large, and while the pager system eliminated the trailing wait lines, there were now trailing lines waiting for a pager. It did not take long, though, for students to realize that if they were waiting for a pager, they would be more than likely waiting for several hours, and eventually, the trailing wait lines for pagers went away. One complaint that surfaced was that the pager's beep was too loud and could not be adjusted by students or desk staff. In a library, noise levels matter, unlike a restaurant. Desk staff would encourage those with pagers to avoid the designated quiet study areas. There was never a good solution to this issue. Students are clever and quickly found a way to circumvent the 4-hour loan policy with the pagers by requesting a pager before their current room occupancy expired. There were also instances where a group member would request a pager to ensure that one's group had a backup room option. While the pager system indeed alleviated much stress for the desk staff, it now meant that they had to be more alert to who was checking out a pager or group study room key, to minimize the potential of individuals taking advantage of the system. Since desk staff rotate shifts, the ability to police student usage nearly becomes impossible.

While the intention is not at all to bore you to tears with detail, as mentioned earlier, the devil is in the details, and the greatest lessons learned came from working through the details. The TAMU Libraries found that cataloging the pagers and checking them out to patrons was the best way to keep track of them. By cataloging each pager, we ensured that pagers would be returned, especially if a student decided he or she no longer needed a group study room. There were occasions when students would return to their dorm, for example, and forget that they had a pager. Recall that one of the criteria for the pagers was their broad signal range. We quickly learned that this was actually not beneficial. Because the transmitter range was too broad (extending nearly half a mile), students would not receive the out-of-range signal if they returned to their dorm room with the pager. Furthermore, the beep was often inaudible if the pager was in their backpack or, worse, if they left their room without their backpack at all.

The pager model also increased the complexity of the service counter work flow. The process for issuing a pager required checking it out, plus recording the transaction on paper and noting the pager number, the time it was issued, and the times it was paged. Once the pager was returned, it was checked back in, reset in its corresponding tower location, and again noted in the paper log. When the student came to the desk after being paged, a group study room key was then checked out to them. The process did not take a long time, but it did require paying close attention and having at least two desk staff during peak times.

One popular question with the pagers became "How long is the wait?" Restaurants also get this question, yet unlike restaurants, libraries do not seem to have a good way to judge wait time. And unlike restaurant staff, desk staff cannot glance around to see if anyone is nearly done to make a judgment call. Desk staff would on occasion attempt to give an estimated wait time, but if it was not accurate, students would become unhappy and frustrated. Instead, desk staff answer the question by telling students where they place on the wait list. Students seem satisfied with that response.

Technical difficulties also emerged with time and with repeated high usage of the pagers. The biggest challenge was keeping the pagers charged during peak times when there was high turnover. The pagers simply would not sit in the charging tower long enough. Basically, the pager would go silent. There was absolutely no warning to desk staff or students that it was losing power. Eventually, a student would get tired of waiting, and sometimes the wait was lengthy. When the student felt that the wait time had just been too long, he or she would return to the service desk to then find out that the pager was not working. The desk staff would then manage the request individually and personally to ensure that the next available room went to that student. Another technical difficulty was the occasional interference with other campus signal frequencies. The pager signal would be disrupted and result in a limited transmission range. Students were then advised to remain in the building, therefore eliminating their ability to move about neighboring buildings more freely. Finally, after nearly 4.5 years of service, pagers simply began to die. They had run the course of their technical life and in spring 2012 were officially retired.

BEYOND PAGERS, BEYOND ROOMS

With the official retirement of the pagers, the TAMU Libraries are exploring an online group study room reservation system, again mirroring another customer service industry—hotels. Students now have the ability to check for availability, choose a preferred room, and be in more control over their time by going directly to their reserved room without checking out a group study room key.

Nevertheless, the utility of the pagers has not gone away. There are other high-demand resources that could be better managed with the pagers, such as print course reserves, laptops, equipment, and computer workstations. The University of California–San Diego Libraries utilized pagers for their print course reserves and found them to be an effective tool (Goodson, Christensen, Elliott, & Lowery, 2009).

As I said earlier, librarians love data. The use of a technology such as pagers gives an opportunity for future studies. An analysis of wait times against customer satisfaction and the perceived expectation to the real outcome would be an interesting endeavor. One would think that customer service satisfaction would increase with a decrease in wait time. The use of pagers did not actually decrease wait times at all, and still the perception was improved customer service. A second interesting analysis would be to compare a corporate service industry to a public nonprofit industry. What motivation or incentive is there to decrease wait times at a nonprofit solely to increase customer service satisfaction when there is not necessarily a tie to a for-profit, "time is money" mission? Specific to the TAMU, an analysis would be worthwhile comparing the pager model against the new online room reservation model and the effect on customer service satisfaction and wait times.

CONCLUSION

Libraries are about service. And while popular opinion may predict that books are being replaced by electronic works and that libraries are irrelevant, this is simply not true. The library as a place is still relevant, as evidenced by the growing demand for more study space. Libraries are at the threshold of innovation and creativity. Through the use of relatively simple technology such as pagers, service is improved by effectively and fairly managing a high-demand resource. Libraries stand to benefit by continuously looking at other industries for innovative solutions, and future studies are needed for this exploration.

REFERENCES

Gardner, S., & Eng, S. (2005). What students want: Generation Y and the changing function of the academic library. *Portal: Libraries and the Academy*, 5, 405–420.
Gonzalez, A. (2012). Effective management of high-use/high-demand space using restaurant-style pagers. *Journal of Access Services*, 9(2), 51–65.
Goodson, K., Christensen, M., Elliott, S., & Lowery, A. (2009). Getting buzzed in the library: The use of restaurant-style pagers for reserves checkout in an academic library. *Journal of Interlibrary Loan, Document Delivery, and Electronic Reserve*, 19, 117–129.

Howe, N., & Strauss, W. (2000). *Millennials rising: The next great generation.* New York: Vintage Books.

Mosley, P. A., Carter, H., Desai, S., & Arant-Kaspar, W. (2007, June). *Study rooms and restaurant-style pagers.* Juried poster session presented at the American Library Association Annual Conference, Washington, DC.

Sheesley, D. (2002). The Net Generation: Characteristics of traditional-aged college students and implications for academic information services. *College and Undergraduate Libraries, 9*(2), 25–42.

7

Service Delivery Chains as a Strategy for Improving Library Customer Service

JOHN HUBER
J. Huber & Associates

Many believe that reduced budgets can lead only to reduction in customer service capability. Without a proper plan and strategy, that certainly can result. However, if you squeeze unnecessary waste out of your service delivery chain (SDC)—and, therefore, your costs—customer service will actually improve. Many of my clients can testify to this philosophy: libraries such as Pikes Peak (Colorado) Library District, Mid-Continent (Kansas) Public Library, Tulsa (Oklahoma) City County Library, Ottawa (Canada) Public Library, and many more. For this chapter on best-practice strategies for customer service, I focus on one of my favorite libraries: a two-branch library system in Carrollton, Texas. Carrollton Public Library (CPL), 20 miles north of Dallas, has a collection of 184,000, circulates 750,000 items, and supports a staff of 37.5 full-time equivalents while serving a population of 121,000 residents.

For the past 12 years, I have broadcast to libraries across the country my philosophy that reduced costs can actually improve customer service. My "lean library" workshop is one way that I accomplish this. In 2011, I conducted a series of workshops for the Northeast Texas Library System. Many representatives of the Dallas community libraries attended, including our focus library, Carrollton Public. The workshop provided the participants an introductory understanding of the power of lean library management and SDCs, which I explore later in this chapter. The workshop introduced the following best-practice service improvement concepts:

- Lean is like a smooth flowing river (the River Lean), as opposed to an erratic river (the Snake River). The River Lean has smooth banks and steady, flowing water with clear sailing ahead. The Snake River, (in which most organizations find themselves) has twists and turns (poor flow), destructive hidden rocks (inefficiencies), and periods of dry and muddy river beds (imbalances) followed by intense flooding (peak loads).

- Lean sees your library as a series of SDCs, not segmented departments or staff.
- Lean teaches us that measurements drive and feed your service performance; therefore, what you do not measure must not be important.
- Lean knows that waste exists in every service process that a library supports.
- Change resistance to lean service improvements can be overcome if your metrics align your staff with service performance, as opposed to budget reductions.
- Lean shows us that service improvement leads to dramatic cost reduction.
- Success can be achieved by following the library lean tools and methodology.

Two major factors drove CPL to attend this workshop. First, when it comes to reducing wasteful costs, Carrollton's city council is a very serious group. As far back as 2002, the city implemented what it called a "managed competition" program, whereby each of its service groups is targeted for a competitive review. Of the 11 groups reviewed thus far, 4 were outsourced. CPL was next on the managed competition list. You can only be impressed with Carrollton's managed competition program. In the words of Tom Guilfoy, director of managed competition for the City of Carrollton, "Carrollton's 10-year-old 'managed competition' program has resulted in $30 million in various one-time and on-going savings fund over the years (out of a general fund budget of $74 million)."

Second, to make things even more exciting, just 5 miles up the road, the Farmers Branch city council and mayor sparked controversy when they turned over the management reins of their one-branch community library to a for-profit group. Carrollton knew that to survive as a management group, it had to not only reduce cost but improve customer service at the same time. In the words of Lynette Jones, CPL public services supervisor, "staff had witnessed other city departments work through the process and either win (be declared substantially competitive) or lose (get outsourced to a private vendor), and everyone knew that we were playing for high stakes (life and civilization as we know it)."

Carrollton and Farmers Branch are not alone. City managers across the country are asking the same questions: "Can our library leaders do more with less? Can they improve customer service with less cost?" I can testify that library managers across the country are more than up to the challenge, and the story of CPL is a perfect example.

After the Northeast Texas Library System workshop, Carrollton's leadership team approached me (as well as many other Dallas area community libraries) and requested a follow-up workshop that would focus just on its library. We did not waste much time. I arrived for the follow-up workshop just a few weeks later. The CPL team proved to me how motivated it was, as team members were fully prepared. They had developed the requested flowcharts and video of our first targeted SDC: the customer holds process. To my surprise, two members of the Carrollton city government joined the workshop (Beth Bormann, assistant city manager for leisure and support services, and Tom Guilfoy, managed competition director). This participation reflected the city leaders' commitment level and was invaluable to the workshop's success.

During this workshop, Carrollton taught me a very valuable lesson in best-practice service improvement. We reviewed the library lean methodology, service objectives, and flowcharts, and with great anticipation, we sat down to watch the video. I have worked with many groups and cultures, and I have found that while process steps are fairly similar from one library to the next, organizational cultures are not. This difference becomes the most apparent when the groups watch their SDC videos. It is like seeing yourself in a mirror for the first time. I have seen groups become defensive; I have seen groups deny what they are seeing; I have even seen groups put a figurative bag over their collective heads (hoping to hide from the problem). I have never seen a group like Carrollton: it laughed hysterically. Their responses were "I didn't know we were doing that!" "I do that same thing, after you do!" "OMG, why are we doing THAT?"

It was hard for me to hear all the comments, because they were overpowered by shrieks of laughter. But it was not just laughter; ideas to improve and attack the waste they saw on the screen flowed so fast that amid my own laughter, I had a hard time writing them all down. (One participant who had joined the workshop from another nearby library whispered to me, "Can you get me some popcorn—this is just too entertaining.")

The CPL workshop was in direct contrast to a workshop I conducted a few months later. This group started out fairly enthusiastic; however, as we watched the video, I could see the group's body language change: members began retreating into their protective shells. The look on their faces was one of fear. This group was afraid of getting in trouble and being singled out for the waste that was unfolding on the screen. Their fear trumped any desire to attack this waste, which leads me to our first best-practice service lesson— laughter, not fear, should guide your service improvement efforts.

After the workshop, CPL went to work preparing for its managed competition review, starting by establishing its driving objectives:

- To be declared "substantially competitive" (i.e., avoid being outsourced)
- To look at every procedure and process, analyze them, and find ways to improve
- To leverage technology in the most cost-effective way possible

SERVICE DELIVERY CHAINS

In the words of Cherri Gross, former CPL director,

> We began our managed competition process by conducting a SWOT analysis (strengths, weaknesses, opportunities, and threats) assigning an EOT (employee operations team) and then using Mr. Huber's methodology to evaluate each one of our SDCs. Smaller teams were assigned a SDC and an action plan was developed. The library management team prioritized the services in the action plan.

Let us briefly explore this best-practice concept: SDCs represent the series of process events (from beginning to end) that provide an end product or service to your customer. As summarized in my book *Lean Library Management,*

> While libraries are organized and managed within departments or functions, this does not truly reflect the actual flow of services you provide. In fact, department walls can actually inhibit your ability to provide low-cost, high levels of service. The survival of any business lies in its ability to effectively service their customers and to do it in the shortest time at the lowest costs possible. When the separate processes that link together to create this service are separated and managed separately by different groups, the forest can easily be lost among the trees. Library Lean teaches us to ignore the department walls and organizational chart and recognize and document what the true service delivery chain is.

Table 7.1 provides a list of SDCs that CPL defined, measured, and attacked.

To improve the service and cost performance of these SDCs, Carrollton's leadership team launched formal project charters divided among SDC teams. The project charter task form created by Carrollton's organizational development department guided each team to define its purpose, scope, and desired results. The teams were also required to use sound project management tools, including task lists, deadlines, and clear assignments and responsibilities.

Table 7.1. Carrollton Public Library: Targeted Service Delivery Chains

Customer holds	Signs and verbiage
Customer service desk	Grant acquisition
New book	Computer assistance
Self-check	Circulation
Security	Weeding/disposal of withdrawn
Staffing/scheduling	Phone
Customer notification	Donations
Materials returns check-in	Volunteer
Lost and paid	Customer and staff emergency
Fax	New books in transit
Easy books	Story time
Scanning and printing	E-book
Magazine	Coffee shop
Newspaper	Teen services
Computer class	Adult programming

Performing their SDC analysis over a period of about a year, the teams incorporated J. Huber & Associates' Library Lean Project methodology (Huber, 2011; see Table 7.2).

Table 7.2. Lean Service Delivery Chains (SDCs): Methodology

Sequence	Action Item
I	Identify your service delivery chains (SDCs) as well as your SCD performance objectives.
II	Prioritize your improvement focus and assign cross-functional teams to these priority SCDs. (Carrollton decided to attack them all!)
III	Flowchart your SDC so that everyone on the team understands how the process works.
IV	Measure how the SDC is performing in terms of service, costs, safety, and quality.
V	Conduct benchmarking and competitor analysis to challenge "in the box" thinking.
VI	Challenge every step of the process to improve service lead times (speeding the flow of the river).
VII	Video key process links to examine the waste. Attack waste through brainstorming sessions.
VIII	Prioritize your improvement ideas.
IX	Perform a cost-benefit analysis of your new design concepts.
X	Pilot your ideas to ensure success.
XI	Implement performance metrics to ensure that the SCDs meet your performance objectives.
XII	Attack all performance gaps again and again.

SUCCESSFUL OUTCOMES

It is beyond the scope of this book to provide a complete accounting of all the team's accomplishments and project deliverables. However, as it is the focus of this series to identify best-practice tools that you can apply in your library environment, I would like to provide a few highlights of CPL's SDC teams accomplishments.

CUSTOMER HOLDS SDC TEAM

During my library workshops, I introduce a tool that I developed called the *holds label solution*. The concept uses my "first touch rule" of library lean, which states, "If you can perform a task the first time you touch something, do it, because it will eliminate tasks throughout the rest of the process." The holds label solution accomplishes this by combining the pick list, in-transit slip, and the holds slip into one removable label. In other words, the staff person pulling the hold uses the label to find the book on the shelf and then applies that label onto the spine of the book the first time the book is touched. This eliminates the in-transit slip and holds slip activities later in the process. CPL embraced the concept by launching the Customer Holds SDC Team. As a result the team freed up 256 clerical hours per year while reducing the time to get the book to the holds shelf by 25%.

NEW BOOK SDC TEAM

CPL's most dramatic impact on service as well as cost came from the New Book SDC team. This team reduced new book delivery times by 95% (from 2 to 3 months to 1 week) and reduced staffing by 50% (six staff employees to three). Specifically, it expedited cost-effective vendor delivery of cataloging and processing services, reduced manual invoice data entry through electronic ordering and invoice consolidation, and implementing vendor-generated bar codes and list prices in records. Vendor shipments were also consolidated into weekly deliveries.

CUSTOMER SERVICE DESK SDC TEAM

The Customer Service Desk SDC team soon discovered there was much more to its service chain than just one overall flow. To fully define customer service, the team identified additional SDC flows, as shown in Table 7.3.

Table 7.3. Customer Service Desk's Service Delivery Chains: Detail Service Flows

Study room	Check-in
Library cards	Paying fines
Holds pickup	Print cards
Guest pass	Computer access request

Using the library lean best-practice tools of flowcharting, videotaping, and brainstorming, the team soon discovered that its current two-desk approach (one for circulation support and one for information/reference support) created a great deal of waste, including duplication of tasks, separation of staff during peak load times, customer confusion, as well as congestion in the main traffic areas. The videos revealed many opportunities for improvement. The team identified many service benefits by consolidating the two desks into one—specifically, it

- eliminates customer confusion while providing a better service experience,
- improves peak load service response by better utilizing cross-trained and consolidated staff,
- increases staff productivity by eliminating duplicative steps, and
- facilitates productivity of staff's "off-line" duties.

The one-desk concept improved productivity by 33% while eliminating extra walking time and congestion for both the customer and the staff.

VOLUNTEER SDC TEAM

CPL believed that it could better leverage staff by increasing the use of community volunteers. An initial step was to benchmark against other libraries in the area. Table 7.4 presents their findings.

The gap between CPL and comparison libraries showed potential for improvement. As a result, the staff reenergized the process by creating a collaborative citywide volunteer effort. Specifically, Libraries, Parks, and Animal Services are now working with Citywide Workforce Services to create a cooperative volunteer program for the city. CPL expects to soon close the gap between themselves and its benchmark libraries.

Table 7.4. Volunteer Service Delivery Chains Team

Benchmarking Data	Carrollton	McKinney	Denton	Richardson	Plano	El Paso
Volunteer hours library	1,514	2,866	8,065	7,493	4,027	5,503
Population served, 2009	119,097	135,000	113,383	99,223	261,350	649,121
Population, %	1.27	2.12	7.11	7.55	1.54	0.85
No. of branch libraries	2	1	2	1	1	3
No. of museums	1	6	3	0	1	3

CHILDREN'S SDC TEAM

The Children's SDC Team identified the need to evaluate its current strategies against a for-profit competitor; after all, that is what the managed competition program is all about. The group researched local bookstores to see how they support children services. The team found that the bookstores had advanced sign-up, shorter programs, Spanish programs, craft and coloring, use of Nooks, kids clubs, and paid book performers.

The team did not stop there. It moved forward by benchmarking itself against the local school district's curriculum. As a result, the Children's SDC Team created new and innovative programs more aligned with customer and community needs. CPL believes this will result in better story times that will have a lasting impact on the children and their parents.

The following provides additional highlights of other SDC team accomplishments:

- The Grant Acquisition SDC Team formed by library staff and parks/recreation staff banded to form the Leisure Services Grant Team. The library applied for five grants in fiscal year 2011–2012 and received funding from two of those sources.
- The e-Book SDC Team added 515 targeted offerings.
- The Reference SDC Team targeted and added 24 homework and medical virtual reference books to enhance 24/7 research assistance.
- The Computer Class SDC Team added 88 volunteer-based computer lab and training programs for Microsoft Word, Excel, and PowerPoint, as well as resume writing and job hunting.

On March 6, 2012, CPL was declared substantially competitive. In the words of Carrollton's city manager, Leonard Martin, "Anyone can do more with more. It takes a leader and manager to do more with less. And that's where our [library] people are." The following summarizes the best-practice lessons that we can take from CPL's lean/managed competition efforts.

- Leaders must be passionate about making libraries "lean," not because they have to, but because it is responsible use of community resources.
- Government organizations must recognize that they are competing for the right to service their customers at the lowest competitive cost. If they cannot, somebody else will.
- Everyone, from the director down, needs to be on board. It is extremely important that everyone know that this is not about the individual's needs; it is about library services as a whole and what is best for the customer.
- An organization's driving objectives should be top-down driven and bottom-up supported. In the words of Tom Guilfoy, "Whenever you're in a change process, everybody needs to be pulling in the same direction. It's not about who is right or wrong; it's about what we need to do to be competitive."
- SDCs should be your first step in understanding your organization, and they should drive your team efforts to streamline and improve services and, as a result, reduce cost.
- The lean library management methodology is a proven approach to improve services and reduce costs.
- Teams should seek input and obtain ownership from front-line staff who best understand the bottlenecks and problems that affect service.
- Project management tools such as Carrollton's project charter form and task list, service performance goals, targeted milestones, clear assignment of responsibility, and regularly scheduled status reports are critical to success.
- Videotaping your processes is an invaluable tool to expose hidden waste in your process.
- Teams should be cross-functional to reflect all parts of the SDC.
- During the allotted "pilot" period, resistance will be strong, so be firm about any changes. Learn from the pilot, improve what has been changed, but never go backward—always move forward.
- Finally and perhaps most important, laughter is your first and best tool to attack waste, improve service, and reduce costs.

John Huber

REFERENCE

Huber, J. J. (2011). *Lean library management: Eleven strategies for reducing costs and improving customer services.* New York: Neal-Schuman.

8

The Buzz on Patron Service

SHANNON HODGINS HALIKIAS
The Lisle Library District

Have you ever visited the library to use a computer and found all of them full? In the days of increasing demands on technology, this is a frequent scenario as libraries seek to provide an ample amount of technology for patrons that use the library for educational, communication, and work-related purposes. This scene is happening all across the United States as demand increases, and for the Lisle Library District, we saw our technology demand increase by 20% between fiscal years 2010 and 2012. In our last fiscal year, 52,895 Internet sessions were recorded on the PC stations, with thousands of additional wireless sessions.

Patrons are also increasingly stretched for time as they multitask and use the library for more than one function. Oftentimes, they may want to check out a movie, attend a program, and use resources all on the same visit. During their visit, they would like to get the most from their library with the least amount of constraints possible. These constraints can include waiting or policies that are a point of frustration. To reduce constraints and strengthen the comfort level of our physical space, utilization and technology were key for the Lisle Library District.

Almost every librarian can also attest to the increased focus on patron satisfaction as we compete with consumer-based organizations. Intelligent consideration of what may be feasible and applicable in a library environment is important as we continue to evolve our services and resources. Sometimes looking outside our walls can help us bring some of the best ideas inside. Lisle is leaping forward in more ways than one by creating fabulous social media initiatives, beginning with circulation of e-readers in August 2012 as well as installing a new teaching and learning desk called the Reader's

Hub. Technology is viewed as an extension of current library services and resources as well as another arm of expanding means to connect with patrons.

ABOUT LISLE LIBRARY DISTRICT

The Lisle Library District is located in Lisle, Illinois, and has a service population of almost 29,000 users. The 29,500-foot facility was built in the 1980s and has undergone minor renovations to stretch the interior utilization and extend the life of the facility. We currently offer computers for public use in both the adult and youth services departments, which are located on different levels of the building.

Our population is one that values library services, with a circulation at slightly over half a million and a per capita checkout rate of 38 per patron. The demand for technology resources continues to grow as patrons need computers for school, job seeking, information, and communications. We offer standard PCs, wi-fi throughout with wireless printing, copiers, and a wealth of information resources. Like many libraries, we have seen a significant increase in both library usage and technology demands as a challenging economy has drawn many patrons to explore what the library has to offer.

Our community is a varied and interesting mix of demographics as it relates to age, interests, expectations, education, and affluence. Lisle has residents that are deeply invested long-term citizens with a bookcentric traditionalist viewpoint of library services, paired with highly affluent and educated technology-savvy residents that want the latest and greatest in research, database, and media resources.

A key challenge for our facility is working with a 1980s building that is not geared for technology. The current placement of our computer stations is awkward, as we do not have a designated computer lab. Computer stations are located in the immediate vicinity of the reference desk and in the midst of the periodical and nonfiction collection. Due to space constrictions, there is only a small amount of space for computer stations (Figure 8.1).

Plans for the coming year include restructuring the periodical sections to accommodate additional computer stations and increased room for each patron's work area. We hope to accommodate these changes without heavy construction or loss of print materials, yet we will be working with very limited areas, and placement selections will be crucial. Our limited space challenges and tight areas ultimately became a factor in deciding to go with the new buzzer-style notification system for our print and Internet management. As we honed into selecting the CASSIE system with additional features, our space challenges played into the final decisions to a significant degree.

Figure 8.1.   Computer stations at the Lisle Library District.

FIX IT IF IT'S BROKEN

Our decision to migrate to another system was prompted by reoccurring issues with a print management system that had been in place for a number of years. In 2011, an upgrade to this system sent the network askew, prompting numerous service interruptions. These frequent issues posed not only a challenge to providing adequate technology resources but also a time burden on our limited information technology (IT) administration capability. Most libraries can attest to moments when the phone is ringing, a project is underway, a staffer needs a question answered, the library is packed, and suddenly, four computers go out at once and a patron cannot retrieve his or her print job. These triage moments are truly a test to our ability to manage resources, control stress, and keep a positive outlook!

Like many libraries of our size, we have staff members that perform multiple duties. Our IT administration is managed by the assistant director, Kathy Seelig, with supplemental assistance of an outsourced consultant. Stability in our resources became a pressing issue as, suddenly, problem management of network issues was a daily frustration. Seelig manages approximately 40 computers throughout the building in addition to assistant duties, a heavy load even for a seasoned professional. When problems begin to mount at an increasing rate, it became a point of frustration for patrons and a huge barrier to good service. When a patron needs a computer now for a resume, he or she doesn't have the time or patience to understand why a resource may not be available.

After the upgrade, we had commonplace and frequent issues, such as random losses of connectivity, loss of data, and reoccurring crashes with our PCs. Without rhyme or reason, multiple PCs would lose service in the middle of sessions, prompting patron dissatisfaction. Multiple tactics were tried to solve the problem, including uninstalling, building PCs from scratch to make sure that no malware was involved, and having on-site visits from the company's technical support. After tracking 22 days of issues, we began searching for new solutions that would work well with our network and needs.

When assessing needs for a new print management system, our focus narrowed to several criteria:

- Effective use with our network and Polaris
- Sophistication of resources to enable multiple user groups with additional variables
- Reasonable costs, including any software and transition costs
- Ease of use for our patrons
- Stability in system
- Ease of administration

RESEARCH AND DECISIONS

Seelig began a research process to explore other options that would work well with our system. She asked other local libraries for recommendations on systems that worked well for their patrons, and the CASSIE system by Librarica was mentioned. A local library in our vicinity spoke highly of the system, indicating that it had used the general print management system with success.

Seelig attended the annual Polaris User Group Conference in Dallas in October 2001 and was able to meet one-on-one with vendors to fully explore the capability of the system. As Librarica is based out of Dallas, it was well represented at the conference. A rich discussion of performance, potential challenges, and network needs was held to explore the possibility to applying the system to Lisle. Technical questions were explored to fully understand the impact on our network and hardware configurations.

To allow access to our computers in the library, we had completely removed the defunct system and were without a time, reservation, or print management system, and we resolved that we needed to make a decision rapidly. Due to the information that we had received so far, we decided to pursue CASSIE as our top runner for a new system.

CASSIE TAKES THE LEAD

Our prior system had required a SQL server to manage the PCs; however, the new CASSIE system from Librarica did not. This would result in a less complex setup that would be easier for internal management and future upgrades. Once we determined that a new server or expensive equipment would not be required to transition, we were extremely pleased with cost projections.

The licensing process was attractive, as the library would need to purchase only the actual number of licenses needed. This tabulated to a total of 21 stations, plus a designated signup station. We would also have the ability to install the same number of administration programs on staff PCs without incurring additional costs. As we added additional stations, we could add licenses as needed, as opposed to having to buy a group block.

CASSIE allows a variety of variations in reservation services and waiting lists. A key feature was the visual management function that allows our patrons to use it with a user-friendly graphical interface, the capability of multiple languages for instructions as needed by patrons, and staff members' management of the system from their own work stations.

The system itself seemed easy to utilize, which would make the transition easier for IT administration, staff, and patrons. The CASSIE manager software would be installed on an internal web server that allowed a fairly simple setup system configuration as well as authentication parameters. CASSIE would use the SIP protocol to check against our Polaris patron database. In addition, we could import our current users and any monetary amounts in their accounts from our former system to CASSIE. This gave us a strong sense that the patrons' satisfaction rate would be higher as their transition impact would be minimal.

Costs were assessed for the system at a total of $5,507. A breakdown of the system shows that $3,187 provided for a total of 21 users, including 1 manager. This cost also included one full year of technical support. As we determined that we were attracted to the pager system, an additional $2,329 was dedicated to provide for 10 restaurant-style buzzers, one paging system, and one station charger. Future anticipated charges for the system will require approximately $500 per year for technical support

A comparison from our old system shows that the installation several years ago cost $8,748. By changing systems, we lowered our ongoing technical support costs from $1,965 to $500. This showed that the system would actually pay for itself in cost savings for technical support in approximately 4 years. Though costs were certainly a factor, the ease of use, the stability, and the enhanced comfort of patrons by the new pager system were the driving factors for selection.

PROJECT INSTALLATION

The conversation to CASSIE was relatively smooth, with minimal service interruptions to patrons and a short learning curve for staff. The Librarica technical support staff were readily available and knowledgeable about the product. To help staff acclimate to the system, we set up a bank of test computers in the director's office for preliminary tinkering. This was followed by a demo for department directors as well as technical specifications.

Prior to installation, we contacted our prior vendor to pull in the financial accounts on file for patrons. This stage of the project required testing and adjusting to set up the information in a format needed by the new CASSIE software. To give the IT staff ample time to make installations and testing, we closed access to our computers for approximately half a day. Our wi-fi connections were still available, though we restricted printing during this duration. To inform patrons in advance, we notified them through sign, web-page, and social media that our computer resources would be limited during this installation period. Staff members were prepared with directions to other local libraries that would allow for technology access.

We set up the CASSIE manager software and ensured that it connected with the Polaris database and that the previous accounts were available with any amounts and credit balances. Once testing of the account balances was completed, the extensive process of installing CASSIE on all of our stations began (Figure 8.2). This process took approximately half a day and proceeded smoothly, with no technical difficulties.

Prior to launch, we provided a demonstration to staff and followed with a printed tip and information sheet. One additional mini-meeting was held to provide a demonstration, and proficient staff took the opportunity to train other staff members that had not been able to attend the demo. Overall, there were fairly few complications in training staff, and we felt that they easily ac-climated to the system. There was a fairly low rate of change anxiety among the staff, as they were ready for a stable system that caused less disruption in services.

The features of the system were truly exciting for us and have been well received by the patrons. We felt as though this was one system that had extras that we frequently see in a business, though not necessarily in a library. As

Figure 8.2. CASSIE reservation station with buzzers.

Lisle will be focusing on increasing the usability and comfort of our facility, we found the usability features to be a perfect match for our strategic goals.

PRINT MANAGEMENT

The ability to manage our current print setup and reconfigure as we grow was an attractive feature of CASSIE. This system offers the flexibility of configuring on a printer-by-printer basis or different charges, depending on your print mode. We had the ability to input print charge changes if we decided to raise, lower, or delete charges as circumstances dictated. In the event of free printing needs, we can input an allotment onto a patron account that will be used before print charges are incurred. We thought this would be very helpful in the case of print errors, as opposed to doing reimbursements of cash or coin.

CASSIE allowed for account transfer that would utilize the patron's existing borrower account, so no additional cards, barcodes, or hardware was required. This allowed for a simple transition that would pose the least impact for our patrons. In our current operations, we utilize the automated payment system, which allows our patrons to deposit a balance on their account and deduct as needed with each print job. This system requires minimal staff assistance for day-to-day printing needs.

At our print release station, print jobs are transmitted to the station from the patron's PC. Jobs are held at the station for a period of 2 hours, which provides ease of use to patrons. At the station, patrons enter their information to view, delete, or print the jobs they have sent. Patrons confirm the amount to be deducted before submitting the final click to print the job.

RESERVATIONS

The ease of use in reservations was an attractive feature for patron ease and comfort. We are able to configure how our access is organized, and we elected to put the assigned waiting list onto our adult department computers only. Currently, we do allow adults to use the computers in the children's department, but naturally, adult users queue into the adult resources as they log-in to the system. If there are immediate openings, the patron may go directly to a computer and begin use without having to use the reservation system. A web reservation interface is available through a web reservation module.

Each library may elect to use either the reservation system for a specific time or computer or a waiting list system. Our library found that a waiting list would provide for the maximum use of our resources. When all computers are full, a patron registers on the control kiosk by using his or her library barcode. When the user reaches the top of the list, he or she is assigned to a computer exclusively for one's use.

WIRELESS PRINTING

Wireless printing is an important component of day-to-day offerings that we provide for patrons. It is commonplace to see patrons working on papers, personal documents, research, and office-related duties in the public library. We are truly America's new office on the go. Having seamless integration of wireless printing was a priority for selecting a good print management system.

The CASSIE system has a companion SPOT program for patron authentication, session control, and printing. Patrons are able to fully utilize the printer stations through the wireless printing, while the library can retain control of payment options to maximize control over printing. The printer does not need to be wi-fi enabled, and we are able to utilize our existing resources. Encryption technology ensures patron privacy for a quality library experience.

STATISTICAL REPORTING

Statistical reporting is extremely important in a library environment where usage, costs, and financial tracking is par for the course of any public service. We found that CASSIE had excellent enhancements to track a variety of system operations. Using these data is important to track our annual statistics and measure performance. The CASSIE program allows for downloading of data and importing into traditional spreadsheet programs such as Excel.

A sample of some of the reports that we felt would be frequently used in Lisle included session usage, total time of computer usage, session lengths, and number of reservations made. Additional reporting features included missed reservations, length of waiting lists, and average waiting time. These reports can be deployed to assess if additional technology resources are needed as we continue to grow. Results can be arranged by time or by a variety of different parameters. The accounting capability is a valuable tool for tracking and maintaining accurate records.

THE BUZZ ON GOOD SERVICE

During our research process, we discovered that CASSIE had a marquee option for patron notification of turns or a new restaurant-style buzzer option (Figure 8.3). The buzzer option had not been part of our initial discussions, as this information was actually not even on its webpage. Once we began to explore the option, it increasingly became an intriguing thought due to our physical layout and current technology limitations. Though this had not been tested extensively in a library environment, we were extremely familiar with the concept. It had an immediate *Wow!* factor for patron convenience and comfort.

At peak hours, we would find our banks of computers full and patrons anxiously waiting for their turn. Other systems currently in action in libraries kept patrons in close range of the computers or constantly eying a clock to see if their turn was approaching. Looking externally to business models was prudent, as patrons are now familiar with buzzers through restaurants and other facilities where they must wait. In a library, it made even more sense, as patrons have the ability to enjoy the collection, resource space, and browsing to a greater degree rather than be tied to only one area of the library.

The pagers are wireless and extremely easy to use. Once patrons sign into the waiting list, they simply take the top buzzer on the stack and are free to move about the library. The buzzers are lightweight and easily understood in purpose and use by patrons. This has facilitated a very easy transition, and patrons have viewed it as a wonderful convenience.

Once it becomes a patron's turn, the buzzer will light up and vibrate readily, alerting the patron to proceed to the computers. We selected the higher-end buzzers, which have the assigned computer number listed on the buzzer, thereby making it extremely easy to understand where to go. The system is remarkably easy, and since installation in June 2012, we have had relatively few patron questions about the system.

Figure 8.3. Library director Shannon Hodgins Halikias.

So far, the results have been a smash hit with our patrons and staff. Our key criteria have been met, and the stability of the system has been excellent. The use of buzzers has been a success, as patrons may now browse the library and maximize their time without having to lurk in the immediate computer area. We feel that the perception of enjoyment in the library visit has increased, as patrons using the computers also no longer feel that they are being hovered over by other patrons or hurried to finish their work. Patrons waiting can now browse, which we hope will also increase the circulation of print materials.

CONCLUSION

Though the system is very new, we feel confident that it will strengthen the perception of a comfortable visit for our patrons (Figure 8.4). The system will ultimately pay for itself in cost savings for technical support while providing stability, ease of use, and enhanced enjoyment while visiting the facility. The verbal feedback we have received so far has been positive, with many patrons applauding the use of external business ideas in the library to increase their satisfaction. As we hope to add additional computers in the library and increase the comfort level of the stations themselves, we feel that this project has begun to move us forward into crafting better experiences overall.

Figure 8.4. Lisle Library District cards. A patron logs in to use the computer with a library card. The patron print account is managed through the library barcode.

As we are one of the first libraries in our region to test the idea of buzzers for waiting lists, we were happy to be a testing ground for this concept. The idea itself is not new, but to bring it into the library for comfort and wait management is new. Libraries are constant innovators in resources, technology, and services, which contribute to our success as a sustaining organization.

9

Make Your Library Fantastic for Homeschoolers

ABBY JOHNSON
The New Albany-Floyd County Public Library

It's a Friday morning during the school year, and we might be crazy because we're holding our breath, waiting to see a deluge of school-age children coming through the doors. We've been planning to try this new program for months, and it's not always easy to get something new off the ground in this community. People are rooted in tradition, and our biggest library events are the ones that have been going on for years. It's winter, and we're wondering if the cold will keep people away, when we see our first family coming up the hallway toward the Children's Room. We breathe a sigh of relief and welcome our first participants to Fantastic Friday, a new program for home-schoolers at the New Albany-Floyd County Public Library.

We've been offering the Fantastic Friday program now since 2010, and it's been one of our best-attended regular programs, filling a definite need within our community. One facet of our library's mission statement is to provide lifelong learning opportunities for all patrons. When I started with the library in May 2009, it became apparent very quickly that we were serving a large homeschooling population and that it wanted more from us. Library staff recognized a number of homeschooling families and had good relationships with them; yet, even though we were offering many programs to our community, we weren't offering any programs or services aimed directly at homeschoolers. I had a feeling that we had a large untapped market, and I went about trying to figure out how we could best serve our homeschooling community.

Reading Adrienne Furness's book *Helping Homeschoolers in the Library* (American Library Association, 2008) gave me a great starting point. I began to talk to our homeschooling patrons, and I found out that there was a great desire for some kind of homeschooling programming from the library.

In August of that year, I was invited to man a library table at a local home-schooling support group's community resource fair. I took advantage of this opportunity to distribute a survey to find out what types of programming local homeschoolers would like to attend and what times worked best for them (Figure 9.1). After considering survey results and having conversations with homeschooling families in our library, we decided to launch Fantastic Fridays in early 2010.

Getting input from our homeschooling families was instrumental in planning how we would offer our program. We learned about special events that were already being held in our community (science fairs, spelling bees, etc.) and when other organizations held regular meetings so that our time wouldn't conflict. To keep it as easy to remember as possible, we chose a meeting time that would be the same each month—the second Friday of the month at 10:00 AM.

We distributed publicity through our normal channels—press releases to the paper, flyers in the library, information on our website—and we passed information to our local homeschooling groups. I joined two local home-schooling listservs to promote our programs and services for homeschoolers and to keep my finger on the pulse of our homeschooling community. Joining the listservs not only let me publicize our programs but allowed me to develop a better collection for homeschoolers by paying attention to the resources they recommend to one another. I also asked my staff to talk up the program to homeschooling families they knew.

All our planning and marketing efforts paid off that first month when we had a crowd of over 20 people attend the program. In our community, that's a great number for any program, let alone something brand new. We knew that we had hit on something big, and we definitely wanted to keep it up. We planned to repeat the program monthly with different topics, and with a great response to the first program, we decided to go ahead with making the second Friday of every month "fantastic for homeschoolers!"

The numbers and feedback for Fantastic Friday have been steady and positive ever since. Offering the program allows us to connect with our homeschooling population in a way that we hadn't before. This regular program brings homeschooling families back into the library month after month, allowing them to form relationships with one another and with library staff. Homeschooling parents are more comfortable asking library staff for help since they have gotten to know us by attending these programs.

In addition to our repeat customers, offering a homeschooler program allows us to quickly connect with new homeschooling families. The library is often a first stop for new homeschooling families, and when they come in to ask about resources or support groups, we are quick to let them know that we have regular programs just for them.

Are you a resident of Floyd County? (Circle one.)
Yes   No

What age group(s) would you most like to have programming for? (Circle all that apply.)
Baby/Toddler (up to 3 years old)   Ages 3–5   Grades K-2 (ages 5–8)
Grades 3–5 (ages 8–11)   Grades 6+ (ages 11+)

What time of day are you most likely to attend a library program? (Circle all that apply.)
Weekday morning   Weekday afternoon   Weekday evening   Weekend

If it depends on the day, please indicate a day and time you would likely be able to attend a library program: _____

Please check the programs that you might be interested in attending: (Check all that apply.)
- Storytime for younger elementary students
- Book discussions (one-time program)
- A book club that has regular meetings
- Craft programs
- Science programs
- Programs open to all ages
- Programs open only to my homeschooling group
- Other (please specify, if you need more room please use back of sheet): _____

How do you hear about library programs? (Check all that apply.)
- The library website
- The library newsletter
- Schedules and/or signs in the Children's Department
- The newspaper
- Word of mouth
- Other (please specify): _____

Would you be willing to participate in a one-time focus group to help library staff plan programs that meet the needs of homeschooling families? If so, please provide contact information (phone number or e-mail address) on the back of this sheet.

Name: _____

Phone number: _____

E-mail address: _____

Figure 9.1.   Homeschoolers programming survey.

AIMS AND OBJECTIVES

We have several objectives for our Fantastic Friday programs, the first of which is to serve a previously underserved portion of our population. According to a report by the National Home Education Research Institute, the number of homeschooled children continues to grow each year. As this population increases, it becomes clear that homeschoolers are a viable target population and libraries should reach out to them just as they would any other segment of the population.

We also aim to introduce homeschoolers to the resources available in the library. Throughout our programs, we highlight and display the many resources that the library has to offer. Book displays and take-home packets showcase books and audiovisual materials related to our monthly topics and to education. We offer tours of the library to new and returning families upon request, and we make sure to point out collections that might be of particular use to homeschooling families, including our parent/teacher shelves with education books, our book discussion sets, and our educational DVDs. Even regular library users may not be familiar with every resource that the library has to offer homeschoolers.

Throughout our interactions with homeschooling families, we emphasize the role that librarians can play in finding resources for lessons and projects. We let homeschoolers know that we're happy to pull books for them on a particular topic, just as we do for the teachers and day cares in our county. We're happy to demonstrate the library's catalog and online databases. By educating parents and children about library resources, we aim to create life-long library users.

Besides providing an educational opportunity for our homeschoolers, Fantastic Friday provides social opportunities for our homeschoolers. We know that today's homeschoolers don't just learn at home—many of them are involved with social groups through Scouts, 4H, and other local organizations. When we welcome homeschoolers to the library for a program, the library becomes a community gathering place, a place to network with other homeschool families. Since the library is often a first stop for new home-schooling families, we have a unique opportunity to connect these families with resources.

ABOUT THE PROGRAM

Fantastic Friday meets on the second Friday of the month during the school year. We don't meet during the summer, since we have many programs for all ages and at all times of day during those months. Now that word has spread about Fantastic Friday, we feel comfortable changing the date occasionally to better meet the needs of our community and our library. Because many of our homeschooling families have multiple children and a wide range of ages, we tailor the program for those five and older. We are as flexible as possible about this, and siblings are always welcome. We leave it to the discretion of homeschooling parents to decide when their children are ready to attend, and we let them know that if they want to try it out, they are welcome to leave the program if their child becomes distracted.

We begin each meeting with the whole group. This gives us a chance to make any announcements that we may have about upcoming programs or to feature new additions to the collection. We always put up some kind of book display, whether it's highlighting resources that homeschoolers may not know about (e.g., our book discussion sets or magazines) or a thematic book display that goes along with that month's program. While we have everyone, we announce the day's activities and what we have coming up for the next month. We always have the sign-up sheet for the next month ready so they can go ahead and register. This has been a useful tool in getting our families back in the door, and we've found that the further in advance that we can plan our programs and get the word out, the better our attendance is.

After our announcements, we either split into groups or head straight into the day's activities. Because we have such a wide range of ages, we try to come up with activities that will appeal to all. Sometimes we split into two groups and have different activities for the younger children and the older children. Sometimes they are related (e.g., two Black History Month activities), and sometimes they're not (e.g., a program about the life cycle of a chicken for the younger group, a booktalk about new books for the older group). Generally, we suggest ages 5 to 8 for the younger group and 9 and up for the older group, but we let parents and children choose which activity is appropriate for them.

We always try to have something for our homeschoolers to take home with them, whether it's a book list of titles we just booktalked or a packet with related resources and activities to explore. If the month's topic is something that piques their interest, we want homeschoolers to have resources to continue to learn at home. We usually include a book list of library titles pertaining to the subject, some kind of activity or recipe to try at home, and a related article that can be accessed through our library's databases.

We have offered many topics for Fantastic Friday over the years. The secret is that a program for homeschoolers can be the same as any program that you offer for your general population. Do you have a successful program that you've offered before or a fantastic school-age program that had low attendance during the after-school hours? Hold it again during a week day and market it to your homeschool population. *Voilà!* A homeschool program! We've even occasionally offered the same program on an evening for the general population and then again on a Friday morning for our homeschoolers.

Community partners can make a big difference in any programs you're planning, and we've found this to be particularly true with our homeschooling programs. We have held Fantastic Friday at the local history museum for a tour of its Underground Railroad exhibit during Black History Month. We have also found that local businesses and organizations are generally happy to donate materials for programs. A local Chinese restaurant donated chopsticks for our Lunar New Year program, and a local orchard donated apples for an apple-themed storytime. Look to your community for experts to present programs such as cooking demonstrations, art instruction, or music recitals.

RESOURCES FOR HOMESCHOOL PROGRAMMING

Our homeschooler programs are very budget friendly, but they can be staff intensive. Luckily, they can be customized to fit the resources you have at hand. We generally use two staff people to run the program, and the staff time spent on preparing for each program varies depending on the topic. When we split the children into younger and older groups, we use one staff person to run each activity. When we have one large group, attendance is usually large enough that it's beneficial to have two staff people running the activity. If staffing is an issue, consider recruiting teen or parent volunteers to help you with your program. Often, homeschooling parents are very invested in what they are doing, and we have found that they are happy to help when asked. We have utilized homeschooled teens to help with some of our craft programs for the younger children, and they are often eager to gain volunteer experience and available at the time of our program.

Another issue that we've had to consider is meeting space. When we split our program into two groups, it requires not only two staff people but two meeting spaces. I book our meeting rooms very far in advance to ensure that we'll have the space we need, and we have also sometimes held parts of the program in our Children's Room, which is open to the public. It's not our first choice, but since the department is generally quiet on our program mornings, it can work in a pinch.

Take-home packets highlight the type of work that librarians can do to help homeschoolers: creating book lists, finding resources, teaching about databases, and so forth. Take-home packets can be a valuable addition to your homeschooler program. They help promote library materials and resources, but they can also be staff intensive to prepare. We consider take-home packets to be an extra-mile aspect of our program: we love to include them if possible, but we know that we may not always have time to prepare them.

With homeschooler programs, a little planning goes a long way. We found that the sooner we decide on topics and start publicizing, the better. Homeschooling families may want to incorporate your program into their lesson plans if they know about it in advance. Give yourself plenty of time to research and prepare activities.

NEXT STEPS

Fantastic Friday has been a very successful addition to our library program offerings, but we are always looking for ways to improve our services to homeschoolers. Starting in fall 2012, we will streamline the format of our program to make it easier to plan and to ensure that it is more effective as an educational tool. One of our homeschooling parents has offered to partner closely with us to make some positive changes to the program. We will plan further in advance so that homeschooling parents can structure lessons around our programs. Our new format puts the focus of these programs on the children learning from and teaching their peers in a group setting.

The planned new format calls for children to read a book and complete a project related to a different topic or literary genre each month. We provide a list of suggested books that we have at the library, and we provide a list of project suggestions, but children are welcome to choose a book or project not on the list. We aim to have a wide range of suggested books and projects so that children of any age can participate at whatever level they feel comfortable.

At our monthly meeting, we hope to put the focus on the work that the children and teens have done instead of focusing on a librarian presenting books and information. This will give the children opportunities to present information to a group and learn from others in their peer group. When we meet, we will divide into an older group and a younger group based on age or reading level. In all our programs for homeschoolers, we emphasize flexibility, and this will continue with our revamped program.

At the end of the school year, we plan to hold a ceremony for the children and parents who have participated in the program throughout the year. Getting recognition from outside the family is important for homeschoolers. Think about all the ways that school children are recognized throughout the year—awards for perfect attendance, grades, athletic performances, and other special achievements are given by most schools. Homeschooling parents, too, need support from others in the community. Outside their own network of homeschoolers, many homeschooling parents are met with confusion or outright disdain. Just as our students need encouragement, parents need encouragement, too.

We are also looking into ways to evaluate our program to make sure that we are getting the results that we want. After we get into the swing of our new format, we plan to survey attendees to find out if the program is encouraging them to increase or diversify their library usage or if it is allowing them to discover library resources they may not have otherwise. We want the program to reflect the interests and educational needs of our homeschooling community, so we will also solicit suggestions for monthly topics.

HOMESCHOOLER PROGRAM IDEAS

Throughout the years, we've offered many different programs for Fantastic Friday. Here are some of my favorites.

Back to Homeschool Party

A Back to Homeschool Party is a great way to kick off the school year in September and help get everyone back in gear. This program also celebrates homeschooling and can provide much-needed encouragement and networking for homeschooling parents. A more casual atmosphere allows homeschooling parents to get to know one another and exchange tips, providing a supportive network for new homeschoolers. Bring out toys and games that you may have in your collection; stock up on healthy snacks; set up a craft table or two; and let your families go to town. Put up book displays featuring a variety of educational books and materials so that parents can peruse while the children meet other homeschooling kids and have a fun time.

If space allows, recruit homeschooled teen volunteers to help supervise children while parents are invited to meet in a separate room to share ideas. Having a library staff member sit in on the parents' meeting can be very helpful for suggesting resources and noting areas that the library's collection can improve. Make sure that children and parents all know where everyone is, and be flexible if a child prefers to stay with mom. Whether parents and children are together or parents are meeting separately, this is a great chance to talk to your homeschoolers and find out how else the library might be able to serve them.

Cooking Programs

Tap into your staff or community resources to find a great cook to demonstrate cooking a dish with the children. Make the program as hands-on as space and resources will allow. When making bread or pretzels, distribute small amounts of dough so that children can practice kneading bread or twisting pretzels. If space does not allow for hand-on activities, invite a chef to demonstrate making a dish, and then parcel out the finished product for tasting. Be wary of food allergies, and keep an ingredient list handy in case anyone has concerns.

Distribute copies of the recipe so that families can try it on their own at home. Pair your cooking demonstration with a book display of cookbooks or cultural books that partner with an ethnic dish. Cooking with children is a great way to reinforce math and science skills, such as measuring, weighing, counting, or even adding fractions.

National Poetry Month Programs

Celebrate National Poetry Month in April by featuring poetry activities for all ages. For the younger group, share a poetry-themed storytime. Read many types of poems, or contact participants ahead of time and ask them to bring a favorite poem to share. Include funny poems, concrete poems, haiku, and other types of poetry. Share Shel Silverstein's poem "Whatif" from *A Light in the Attic*, and invite the group to come up with lines for its own "Whatif" poem. Write down the lines suggested by the children, and then ask for a volunteer to read the group poem aloud.

For the older group, explain book spine poetry and show some examples. Invite the kids to create their own book spine poems. Pull some intriguing titles to get them started, and remind them about searching the library's catalog if they have specific wording in mind. Take photos of the finished results, and create your own "Book Spine Poem Gallery," like the ones seen here: http://www.ninakatchadourian.com/languagetranslation/sortedbooks-sharkjournal.php.

Cultural Month Programs

National cultural months lend themselves nicely to programming, especially for homeschoolers. While many school-age children do cultural month assignments in school, homeschooling families may welcome an opportunity to do the same at the library. Feature books by black authors and illustrators with a related craft for Black History Month, or share Native American tales during November. Partner with a local history museum or cultural center to offer a tour to your homeschooling families. Celebrating cultural months or holidays from around the world can lend nicely to literature pairings and provide an opportunity to feature the diverse titles your collection offers.

Celebrate National Hispanic Heritage month by offering a piñata workshop and featuring books by Latino authors. Blow up balloons, and have families practice making papier-mâché with cut-up newspapers and flour paste. Prepare your own papier-mâché piñatas ahead of time so that families can also decorate one to take home. Recruiting volunteers to help prepare piñatas before your program will make the task much easier! Distribute copies of the instructions so that families can repeat the project at home.

A Trip around the World

Feature a number of countries or cultures in one go by setting up stations around a meeting room or your library. Recruit homeschooled teen volunteers to staff the stations, and provide information about the country or culture to families coming around. Do some research, and print out a small list of talking points for your teen volunteers to share with families. Prep a craft or activity for each station, and set up a small book display featuring books about that country or culture. Print instruction sheets for each craft, and post them at the tables for parents to do with their children. As families arrive, explain that there are a variety of activities and that they may spend as much or as little time at each station as they'd like. Create a passport craft as families' first stop, and have a stamp for them at each table. Although a program like this may require a great deal of preparation, it is easy to run with teen volunteers on the day of the program.

Summer Reading Booktalks

Wind down your homeschool programming year, and kick off your Summer Reading Club with booktalks featuring the new and hot books in your collection. While many school children have teachers, school librarians, and classmates recommend books to them, homeschooled children may rely more on their public librarians for suggestions. Cull a list of your favorites, and encourage children to bring a book they've enjoyed to tell the group about. A book chat program allows children to get some experience talking in front of a group, and kids will often snatch up books that are recommended by other kids. Have the books you talk about on hand for easy checkout, and provide a list of all the books so that kids can come back later to check out books that they may not have grabbed right away. This is a great chance to encourage kids to sign up for the Summer Reading Club or other book clubs that you may be planning. Talk up books that you may be featuring at other programs over the summer or later in the year. Think about including books from state book award lists or recent winners of the Newbery Award, Schneider Family Book Award, or Printz Award.

THINKING ABOUT OFFERING A
HOMESCHOOLER PROGRAM AT YOUR LIBRARY?

The best way to start is by talking to your homeschooling families. If you're not sure if parents are homeschooling, just ask! Find out what kind of programs they might be interested in and what days and times might work. Homeschooling parents may be your best resource to find out what is already being offered in your community and where there are gaps that the library might be able to fill. Homeschooling parents can tell you what resources they lack and what they'd like to see at the library. Parents may be interested in partnering with you, and you may be able to recruit volunteers to help with programs.

Many communities have homeschooling groups, either in person or virtually. Seek out these groups, and let them know about services that the library offers. If your local homeschooling group has meetings, offer to present about library resources, or ask if you can attend to take notes about how the library can meet their needs. Subscribe to local homeschooling listservs, and pay attention to what they're saying. Parents often suggest resources to one another, and that can provide ideas for items to add to your collection. Listservs are also a great way to market your programs and services.

Although homeschooling families may have let you know if there's something that your library lacks, they may have no basis of comparison. They may not know what they're missing, and they may not have a clear idea of what the library can offer them. Don't be afraid to jump in and get a homeschooler program started, even if you don't have every kink worked out. There's always room for improvement, and you can always make changes as you go. Note what works and what doesn't, and don't be afraid to change what doesn't work. If you're not sure, ask your homeschooling families what you can do to improve the program.

Homeschooling families are often very heavy users of the library, and they can be powerful allies in times of budget crises—if you have a relationship with them. With the number of homeschooling families growing every year, the question is not "How can we afford to offer programs for homeschoolers?" but "How can we afford not to?"

Index

About the Editors and Contributors

Lewis Belfont is the head of customer service for the Howard County Library System in Maryland.

Audra Caplan is the former president of the Public Library Association.

Adriana Gonzalez is the coordinator of research services at the Texas A&M University Libraries in College Station.

Charles Harmon is an executive editor for the Rowman & Littlefield Publishing Group. His background includes work in special, public, and school libraries.

Shannon Hodgins Halikias is the library director of the Lisle Library District in Illinois.

John Huber is the chief executive officer at J. Huber & Associates in Tulsa, Oklahoma.

Abby Johnson is the children's services manager at the New Albany-Floyd County Public Library in New Albany, Indiana.

Karen C. Knox is director of the Orion Township Public Library in Lake Orion, Michigan.

Michael Messina is a reference librarian at the State University of New York's Maritime College. He has also worked as a researcher at the Brooklyn

Academy of Music Archives. The former publisher of Applause Theatre & Cinema Books/Limelight Editions, he is a coeditor of *Acts of War: Iraq and Afghanistan in Seven Plays*.

Kiera Parrott is the head of children's services at the Darien Library in Connecticut.

Judi Repman is a faculty member in the College of Education at Georgia Southern University, where she teaches online graduate courses in the school library media program.

Mark Smith is the vice president of West Coast operations for library systems and services for the Riverside County Library System in California.